TOWARD MORAL MATURITY

TOWARD MORAL MATURITY

Religious Education and the Formation of Conscience

by
Rev. Daniel C. Maguire
Rev. David P. O'Neill
Paulette Martin
Sister Frances Mary Myers, S.L.
Brother Andrew C. Panzarella, F.S.C.
Rev. Gerard S. Sloyan
Catherine B. Kennedy
Sister M. Loretta Koley, R.S.M.
edited by Mary Perkins Ryan

PAULIST PRESS DEUS BOOKS

GLEN ROCK, N. J. NEW YORK, N. Y.

TORONTO AMSTERDAM LONDON

The articles in this book first appeared in *The Living Light*, a religious education quarterly published by the National Center of the Confraternity of Christian Doctrine, N.C.W.C., Washington, D.C.

NIHIL OBSTAT:
Rev. James J. O'Connor
Censor Librorum

IMPRIMATUR:
✠ Leo A. Pursley, D.D.
Bishop of Fort Wayne-South Bend

May 9, 1968

The Nihil Obstat and Imprimatur are official declarations that a book or pamphlet is free of doctrinal or moral error. No implication is contained therein that those who have granted the Nihil Obstat and Imprimatur agree with the contents, opinions or statements expressed.

Library of Congress
Catalog Card Number: 68-31046

Published by Paulist Press
Editorial Office: 304 W. 58th St., N.Y., N.Y. 10019
Business Office: Glen Rock, New Jersey 07452

Printed and bound in the
United States of America

Contents

INTRODUCTION 1

The New Morality in Focus 5
Rev. Daniel C. Maguire

Forming Christian Consciences: Some Practical Guidelines for Parents and Teachers 23
Rev. David P. O'Neill

Teaching the Fall as a Stepping-Stone to the Redemption 43
Paulette Martin

Teaching the Meaning of Sin and Salvation 55
Sister Frances Mary Myers, S.L.

Eschatology on the High School Level: Problems and Possibilities 67
Brother Andrew C. Panzarella, F.S.C.

Teaching a Personal Relation to Father, Son and Spirit 81
Rev. Gerard S. Sloyan

Forming the Relevant Community: An Experimental Senior High School Program 101
Catherine B. Kennedy

Studying the Person in His Relationships: An Experimental Senior Religion Program 109
Sister M. Loretta Koley, R.S.M.
Sister Jean Frederick, R.S.M.
Mary Dworak

Can We Form Mature Christians? 131
Rev. David P. O'Neill

BIOGRAPHICAL NOTES 149

BIBLIOGRAPHY 151

Introduction

Several petty thefts in one city a few years ago were newsworthy because in no case was more than $24.50 taken, however much more money was in a till. When the thief was caught, he was asked why he had limited himself to this sum. "Don't you know?" he said, "to take any more would have been a mortal sin."

Almost everyone agrees that this "How far can I go?" legalistic and negative morality is inadequate for today's needs. Moralists are re-discovering the centrality of the law of love, of seeking the other's good, and the consequent need for all Christians to cultivate the virtue of prudence—that is, the habit of making wise decisions—in order to implement love. They are saying, as St. Thomas did a long time ago, that making moral decisions means consulting the teaching of the Gospel and the teaching of the Church, the human and Christian wisdom of the past and present. But it finally means making up one's own mind, asking for the light of the Spirit in doing so.

But when a teacher tries to propose such a morality to adult (and even to some adolescent) audiences, he is met with cries of anguish: "But we weren't brought up that way. We were brought up to do what we were told. We can't take on the burden of making moral decisions for ourselves!"

This deep fear of making moral decisions for oneself, even as a member of the Church with its wisdom and that of mankind at one's disposal, indicates other dimensions of the problem. What one thinks about morality is intimately interwoven with what one believes about the nature of sin, of salvation, of the conditions for entering eternal life—in fact, of the relationship God wants men to have to him. If a person has been taught that what God is concerned with is that he stay out of the state of mortal sin, understood as the effect of a serious transgression against God's law, in order to stay in the state of grace given him at baptism and necessary to enter eternal life, then a legalistic morality logically follows. One cannot help but be terrified at the possibility of making wrong decisions and want some infallible authority to ensure that one does not do so.

But if a person is helped to discover that God is love, that sin is turning away from love, that grace is God's offer of the ability to transcend ourselves in love for others, to overcome alienation and self-centeredness and so to live by the Spirit, that what God wants is that we try to act lovingly, to help one another to the "abundance of life" that Christ came to bring men—then the "new morality" no longer seems so threatening. It begins to seem like an invitation to put away a childish super-ego morality and begin to grow toward human and Christian maturity.

This book, made up of articles taken from *The Living Light,* is intended to open out to catechists and parents some of the implications of this "new" approach to morality and practical ways of communicating it at various levels.

The first essay explains what this "new morality" is, and what it isn't. The second offers very practical suggestions for starting children out right on the long path to moral maturity rather than, as is so often done with the best intentions, crippling and handicapping them from the start. The next two articles, on the Fall, and on sin and salvation, are geared to the grade school level; the one following, on teaching the "Last Things" to the high school level, though the same approaches could be used anywhere. Fr. Sloyan's essay on teaching a personal relationship to the Father, the Son and the Spirit, is of universal application and shows, with almost brutal clarity, that we cannot separate "doctrine" from "morals" and from life. The two next chapters outline actual programs which attempt to introduce high school students to the requirements of mature Christian living. And the final article directly attacks the problems: Is Christianity for children or for adults? If so, is it only an elite?

We hope that this book will prove useful to those who are wondering, both for themselves and for the young people in their charge, "Can we form mature Christians?"

MARY PERKINS RYAN

REV. DANIEL C. MAGUIRE

The New Morality in Focus

The new morality is a complex phenomenon proceeding from multiple sociological, cultural and religious factors. It is also the victim of a bad press. Everyone from barrister to bartender, from bishop to Beatle feels called to expatiate on it in a too definitive fashion. Vocal experts in the field of ethics have sallied forth and added to the muddle with their simplifications. "Love is the only absolute," they proclaim. "Study your situation and do the most loving thing!" Powerfully beautiful statements—and refreshing—but about as helpful for ethical decision-making as "Do good and avoid evil."

Add to this the fact that movies and motels have been basic *loci* for illustrative examples of the new ethic. This has served both to heighten general interest and to give the popularization of the new morality a decidedly sexual accent.

Small wonder that the responsible populace has assumed a dim view of it all. Good people are sure that it is a mini-morality, laxism and hedonism in modern dress. Many see in it the abandonment of moral principles and respect for the wisdom of the past. The teaching role of the Church is obviously threatened, if not dismissed. Anything goes as long as it is done with love! However well-intentioned its purveyors, serious critics feel that the new morality is at root a "hippie" kind of code and the voice of moral chaos.

Meanwhile, back in the tomes, serious ethicists from the various Christian communities have been developing an ethical approach to modern challenges that promises an epochal and enriching renaissance of authentic Christian existence. If its public relations are poor, the theology in its main lines is welcome and heartening. The new moralist departs from the old morality, not because it asked too much, but precisely because it asked too little and, often enough, the unimportant and non-essential things. A better picture of what is happening will be attempted here.

New and Old

The new morality is also old. It is just that the old seems new when rediscovered. Much in this case is as old as the Gospel of Jesus. Somehow or other, Christians have conspired to make the Good News seem bad. The Gospel comes across, especially to the young, as anti-fun, and many do not get much beyond that gloomy indictment. We have failed to communicate the news that Jesus challenged the world to try a new kind of love, a love that was more demanding, more electrifying and more humanizing than any ever known to man.

Not all loves are equally splendored things. Take, for example, narcissistic love. This love takes its name from the mythical youth who fell in love with his own image reflected in a pond. The saddest of men is he who never learns to love anyone but himself. Another kind of love is called *eros*. *Eros* at least gets beyond self and goes out to another. But still it is love with a hook in it. It is an investment that hopes for a return. It goes out to the other primarily because of the delight it finds there. At best, it is a step removed from

Narcissus. Christian love is *agape* and it is an adventure, not an investment. It loves others for their own sake, without any hope of return. The whole business of morality and life, Jesus said, is summed up in this kind of love directed toward God and neighbor.

Jesus' message was this: If you want to love God, then love the way God loves. And God's love goes out to everyone without hope of return, especially to those who are least capable of returning anything: the poor, the beaten, the victims of hate and sinners who are gripped by evil. For one who loves like this, there is no enemy, no foreigner, no stranger. The other has become another self to be loved accordingly. (Obviously, if this is what it means to be a Christian, Christians are rare.)

The stress on love, then, is not an invention of the new morality; it is the substance of the moral teaching of Jesus Christ. The new morality sees in this agapic love an old and neglected challenge; and, as it faces up to the challenge, it rediscovers a second insight of the "old" morality—that Gospel love sometimes requires compromise.

It would seem that a love that called for all one's heart and all one's soul and all one's mind would never deviate from the ideal. Yet, in this sin-ridden and confused world where God has only begun to establish his reign, a compromise is sometimes the truest response of love. Circumstances can be such that it becomes downright harmful and unloving to insist on the ideal. We must always be straining toward the ideal while remaining open to the possibility of loving compromise. This will remain true until God is all in all upon this earth. Until then, love will dictate both rules and exceptions to the rules.

Examples of this are seen in Scripture and in the history of the Church. Jesus said that an ideal love turns the other cheek when struck; yet, when he was struck at his trial, he felt that circumstances did not permit the realization of the ideal, and so he protested. St. Paul exalted the dignity and freedom of persons, and yet he tolerated slavery in the situation of his day. War is an obvious departure from the ideal, and the Church has accepted it. The Gospel calls for permanent marriage, and yet the Church has permitted divorce in the so-called Pauline privilege and in the annulment of unconsummated marriages.

This is perhaps best explained by St. Thomas Aquinas when he discusses the nature of moral principles. The very general moral principles: "Do good; avoid evil. Love God and neighbor," admit of no exceptions. More particularized moral principles (Thomas calls them secondary precepts), do admit of exceptions in the sense that in particular circumstances they will be found non-applicable. Thomas gives a simple example: It is a valid moral principle that we should return borrowed things to their owner. However, if it is clear that the owner now intends to use the property held for him in a destructive fashion, you may decide that the above principle no longer applies. It is still a good principle, but due to circumstances, it ceases to be relevant.

Thomas used this same reasoning to justify the many wives of Old Testament figures. It is a good moral principle that a man may have but one wife; however, special circumstances justified an exception and permitted a plurality of wives.

All of morality is like this, says Thomas. Moral principles are valid most of the time. However, since morality is determined by circumstances as well as principles, special circumstances may dictate exceptions to the principles. This part of Thomas' moral theology had been rather neglected by Catholics until recently.

This does not mean that there are no absolute moral values. The sacredness of life, for example, must always be respected. However, in certain cases, a man may kill. The moral problem is to determine what instances of killing are, because of special circumstances, compatible with a respect for life. With this in mind, Catholic theologians have begun to suggest that we reconsider our stand on abortion. That fetal life must be protected is certainly a sacred moral principle. In certain emergencies, theologians suggest, exceptions to this principle might be morally indicated. Other theologians are applying this type of reasoning to divorce and remarriage. Like war, they argue, divorce is always tragic; but, like war, it might at times also be necessary and moral. The duty for Christians, of course, is to work for conditions where such solutions are no longer necessary.

All of this is basically old theology. What is *new* with the "new" morality? First of all, a lot of new and important emphases, but we shall touch on them singly. Important and new is our deepened understanding of such things as the interdependence of nations, the implications of personhood, the need for mature autonomy, the meaning of marriage and sexuality, etc. Deepened understanding often leads to new conclusions. New also is the complexity of modern life. Moral questions never asked before arise from this complexity. The owner of a little general store in the country a century ago could run on a rather simple code of ethics. Not so the corporation businessman of today, who simply must learn to live with moral ambiguity. As complexity grows, "exceptional" cases multiply. Remembering that love makes its demands through the situations of life, as well as through principles, one should expect much newness in the revolutionized society of today.

Faith and the New Morality

Christian morality is the morality of a believer and a listener. The new morality stresses this. It presupposes a God who speaks, a God who, in creating us, has called us into an unending dialogue with himself. The God of our Scriptures shows that he acts and speaks in our history and calls us each by name. Morality is thus a matter of response, not to a law but to a person. The Christian must have good antennae. "Speak, Lord, your servant listens," is the prayer of a moral man. Finding out what God is doing and, then, joining him is the essence of morality.

A man who has really got hold of this message is one who, in opening the morning newspaper, says: "Let's see what God is up to today!" He doesn't feel that God's will is totally expressed in the missal or the catechism. He senses that God is moving in the world, creating, loving and inviting response. Faith will find him. The news may be a lagging poverty program or a missed opportunity for peace negotiations; it may be riots or pending usury legislation. Christian love will discern what the Lord's interests are and pitch in. The Christian's circumstances may limit his participation, but he is not free to be uninvolved. A Christian who is detached in matters of peace, poverty, or racial disharmony is an apostate. "He who is not with me is against me!" It's as simple as that.

The Social Dimension

"She is an immoral woman." "He was arrested on a morals charge." ". . . for immoral purposes." What are we talking about? Sex, obviously. And it is a macabre tribute to how "hung up" we are on sex that it can become the prime point of reference for the terms moral and immoral. (A caricature of this myopia is provided by the German chaplains who accompanied the troops in the ruthless invasion of Holland, zealously urging the men to avoid the Dutch prostitutes.) Let it be said once and for all: Sex is not the prime moral reality or problem—not even for the young. The new morality is reasserting the social character of the Gospel and the more basic evangelical demands.

The revelation of the mystery of God in trinity points up sharply the social nature of man. "For-ness" marks the inner, personal life of God. Father is seen as existing totally *for* Son. His being is to be *for* the Son and in so doing he gives being to that Son. Father and Son exist *for* and give being to the Spirit. To be is to be for the other. This is the mystery of trinitarian life and it is in the image of this life that we were fashioned. To be a person is to be for other persons. To be for self is sin. It is against this background that we can appreciate the restless love of Jesus for men, especially for men who most needed someone to be for them.

Notice the judgment scene of Matthew 25. Jesus identifies himself with the down and out, and he welcomes to the kingdom those who were for him *in a practical way* when he was a convict, or naked, thirsty, hungry, sick, or alone. And when the comfortably good people protested that they never knowingly slighted the Lord, he replied that they didn't look for him where he was.

We are little inclined to look for God in the rioting Negro, the homosexual, the addict, the mentally ill, the undernourished and starving of the world, in criminals, or in poor, emerging nations. The new morality is reminding us that we must meet God here. And we must meet him effectively—not just as individuals, who avail little in mass society—but with the power of the institutional Church and through the essential medium of national politics. The ancient liturgies prayed to God as "*all powerful* and merciful." It takes power for mercy to be functional, especially today. Another reminder from the new morality.

Law versus Love Controversy

To be really open to the demands of love is complicating and exhausting. Most people opt out. Law provides them a gracious exit. The new morality is not saying that laws are not needed—love cannot function without law! The defendant here is not law but legalism, a misuse of law that frustrates love.

Legalism is a gimmick that people use to get all wrapped up in lesser laws and thus evade the heart of the matter. Those who do this are terribly serious about the lesser laws on which they focus. This helps them to feel justified and to forget how really dishonest they are.

The Old Testament contained the law of love, too. When Jesus asked for a summary of the law, a scribe was able to give him the double commandment of love of God and neighbor. But Old Testament folk also found the legalist escape hatch. An example: The sabbath was to be a weekly day of recollection when work would be put aside and there would be time for worship and rest and meditation. Worship, however, is not so easy, especially when it calls for total commitment to the will of God. So the emphasis came to fall on the "no work" part of the sabbath. And this was enforced with a vengeance to the cruel neglect of love. Way back in the book of Numbers we read of a poor man who dared to gather sticks on the sabbath. The Hebrew legalists stoned him to death. Widows and orphans were exploited without much public shock while the moralists of Israel pondered minute violations of the sabbath rest. They condemned the untying of a knot on the sabbath. Also on the condemned list: putting out a lamp, sewing two stitches (one was permitted), moving objects from place to place. Some felt it was "forbidden work" to defend oneself against attack. Indeed, bodily functions were, as far as possible, to be suppressed! And, just before the time of Jesus, some experts felt that it was wrong to eat an egg laid on the sabbath. (Egg-laying was clearly work and so the principle of cooperation obtained.)

Absurd? Yes, but the old law has no monopoly on such deceits. We still cheat love by being selective in our obedience. The legalist establishes sanctity symbols. By being faithful in these matters, he convinces himself he is a good man. The pharisee gave tithes of all he possessed and thus felt justified. Friday abstinence, Mass attendance and avoidance of contraceptives became the sanctity package of many Catholics, while numerous Protestants chose to concentrate on banning smoking, drinking or Sunday dancing. All of which is a lot easier than loving as Christ did.

The new morality realizes that God can ask more than is asked in a neat code of laws. So does the legalist, but he prefers the code. (After all, it is easier to scruple about fasting than to welcome a Negro neighbor or really forgive an enemy.) But, sadly, his little code makes the legalist a proud and dangerous man. Since he has a simple and set standard of goodness, he is quick and sure about condemning those who do not measure up. "We have a law, and according to that law he must die." Those were the words of a legalist. The new morality recognizes with Augustine and Thomas that the law of Christ is the Holy Spirit who is poured into our hearts. It is primarily the Spirit, not a written code, that tests us; and, since the Spirit's ways are not ours, we are in no position to judge others. Still, we do. That great Christian, H. Richard Niebuhr, summed it up: "We all tend to explain Christianity in such a way as to include ourselves and exclude others." The new morality is a humble morality. It directs us to the back of the temple where a publican admits in God's good grace that he is a sinful man.

A final word on another old strategem of the legalist: the unreal distinction. A modern example: political as distinct from moral. Thus, open occupancy legislation will not be supported on grounds that it is a political, not a moral, matter. Military strategy, too, tends to be lifted to the transmoral realm where it is immune to the moral judgment of the citizenry. The new morality is splashing light on this legalistic skulduggery and reasserting the moral dimension of everything that involves the life and dignity of persons.

The Call to Maturity

The Second Vatican Council, which embodies much of the new morality, has asked the laity to grow up. Of course, we cannot fully blame the laity for their prolonged moral juvenility. They are largely the victims of a paternalistic culture and an overly protective clergy. This, at last, is passing.

The immaturity of children is presumed, as is their need for extensive help in decision-making. Still, the Council says that even children "have a right to be encouraged to weigh moral values with an upright conscience, and to embrace them by personal choice" (*Declaration on Christian Education*, n. 1). Obviously, this is more true of adults. The more maturity, the less need for external direction.

What will this do to Church teaching in the area of morality? Father Springer remarks: "This can only mean that moral teaching in the Church must take more the form of broad guidelines for human conduct and be less the detailed codes of rules it was in the past." Growing up is painful, and people will resist the burden of moral responsibility. For too long they have been looking upon clergy and hierarchy as oracles whence emanated detailed instructions for living. The

Council has tolled the knell of such naiveté. "Let the layman not imagine that his pastors are always such experts, that to every problem which arises, however complicated, they can readily give him a concrete solution, or even that such is their mission" (*Constitution on the Church,* n. 43). It would be equally naive to expect the bishops or the pope to assume the role of conscience for the laity.

What kind of help can maturing Catholics expect from their maturing Church in the future? The Dutch Catechism, provided and approved by the bishops of Holland, gives us an example. To the debated question of what means of birth control are moral, the catechism replies:

> To this question the Council gave no answer. The Council directs all married people to search their conscience and ask themselves whether these methods actually do justice to the great personal values which must come to expression in love relationship and in marriage . . .
>
> Neither a doctor nor pastor of souls pronounces a final judgment of conscience; but respect for life requires that no practice be chosen which can cause serious physical or psychological damage [author's translation].

This is obviously a new way of teaching. The decision about what means to use has been shifted to the married couple; and, since physical or psychological damage is not expected of most contraceptive means, an expanded liberty of choice is offered. How ready the laity are for this responsible freedom remains to be seen. Many, through weakness, will still wait for the decision to be made for them.

Return to Realism

When a pastor of a large suburban parish was told that the new moralists were saying that it is not a mortal sin to miss Mass on Sunday, he panicked and blurted: "They're going too far! That's the goose that lays the golden egg!" Undoubtedly, he had reference to the rich spiritual benefits that attach to weekly worship. The good man's dismay was unnecessary. The new moralists are not playing down the value of Sunday Mass. They do, however, take exception to the theological implications of certain infelicitous expressions such as "obliged to attend Mass under pain of mortal sin." These words easily suggest much that is unreal, as though sin were automatic or something with which you could be punished.

They seem to imply that it is automatically a sin to miss Mass without an important cause. Sin is simply not automatic any more than falling in love or out of it is automatic. Serious sin involves a radical realignment of one's deepest affections. It cannot easily be encompassed in terms of a single act. A single act might indeed climax a substantial change in one's fundamental moral option, and so represent a notable change in the direction of one's life. Missing Sunday Mass without serious reason might or might not represent such a change: (Many a young person who absents himself from Mass has a serious desire for an authentic and meaningful liturgy. Those of us who haven't provided it are more worthy of indictment.)

The seriousness of Church laws does not depend on the will of the ecclesiastical lawgivers. "On the contrary," Father Richard McCormick says, "the lawgiver prescribes the thing, and its gravity is determined by its importance to the Christian way of life. It is the task of the responsible Christian (above all, the specialist) accurately to assess this importance." If no serious harm is done to one's Christian commitment, there is no serious sin. To allege that something is seriously wrong when it does no serious harm is nominalism. The new morality rejects this in the name of realism. Serious Church law may be presumed to embody a serious moral and religious value. It may not be presumed that particular transgressions of these laws necessarily involve a radical repudiation of these values. To be objective and realistic, you must view all the real factors involved and not just the law and the material fact of transgression.

A lack of realism has also pervaded other moral zones. In the field of sexual ethics, for example, the term "mortal sin" has been brandished too glibly as a kind of disciplinary weapon. Certain actions such as "French kissing" have, at times, been labeled mortally wrong with no reference to the harm done, to individual differences, or to the role of conscience. The decisive factor in judging moral guilt in sexual matters has often been the pleasure taken rather than the harm done. This led to frustrating and largely academic examinations of whether or not pleasure was consented to. (The term "ecclesiogenic neurosis" has been used to describe the result of such scrutinia.)

Such a Freudian, anti-instinctual approach to sexual morality is not blessed by the new morality which prefers a realism that is more germane to the biblical outlook. David was not reproached for the pleasure he experienced with Bethsheba but for his exploitation of her. It was his dishonesty and injustice that made his action detestable. The new moralists admire the sexual realism of St. Paul, who appreciated the mysterious unitive power of the sexual act, even when it is performed with a harlot. In a sense, the new morality takes sex more seriously than the old, but without brooding over it as much. Sex is clearly one of nature's finest liturgies–so fine and personal, indeed, that it becomes dehumanizing when it is reduced to mere fun. In questions of premarital sexuality, the burden is on the couple involved to see whether this or that action leads to expressions of intimacy that are dishonest and exploitative since they bespeak a commitment that is not present.

Good people will feel vindicated in their common sense when they hear new moralists saying that a phenomenon such as adolescent masturbation can scarcely be treated in terms of mortal sin. Vatican II has directed moralists to be attuned to the data of the scientific disciplines. Experts tell us that 90 percent of boys go through a masturbatory phase and that this usually represents a development in the integration of sexuality into the personality. Good counseling will help the young to grow gradually out of this narcissistic phase. In the past we often added unnecessary guilt feelings to this sensitive period of maturation. We also managed to put God in the embarrassing position of demanding something that most youth could not achieve. A bitter alienation from religion and a disaffection with authority figures often resulted from this.

Morality as Positive and Creative

Moral theology should be a happy science. It hasn't always been. In fact, it developed into a kind of spiritual pathology, a science of sin detection and analysis. Here again the new morality is corrective. There is no denying that man in his freedom has a right to know the minimal requirements of moral law. But a morality that succumbs to minimalism is like a book on mountain climbing that tells you little on how to climb but concentrates on how far back you can lean without falling. The new morality accentuates the positive. It focuses less on lies and more on the meaning of honesty in interpersonal relationship; it ponders adultery less (and makes it less likely) by exploring how a husband can love his wife as Christ loved the Church and gave himself for it. It is more centered on do's than don't's and sees situations less as problems and more as challenges.

Bergson said there are two kinds of morality: the morality of survival and the morality of creativity. We have no choice but to be creative, since it is with the creator God that we unite in moral action. The morality of survival, in which we have liberally indulged, is obsessed with self-preservation; it is *me*-centered and fear-ridden. And since fear is the bane of imagination and sensitivity, this morality is bankrupt in both regards. One of the greatest sins of Christians has been their dearth of imagination in response to the moral needs of persons and society.

Creativity, of course, involves risk and any creative breakthrough in morality or religion is always resisted by the forces of preservation. Thus it was that Socrates got the hemlock and Jesus, the cross.

Morality as Thankful

It seems that, amid the myriad decisions of each lifetime, two fundamental alternatives are possible: suicide or eucharist. A man may look at life and see the mystery of evil that grips it. He may recoil and say "no," and this is suicidal. Fear, coldness and non-involvement are the symptoms of suicidal man.

The Christian looks at life and says "yes" with thanks. He experiences hope more keenly than evil, and so his mood is eucharistic. He knows that the decision to affirm life, to redeem it and enrich it, can be costly. Jesus said "yes" and gave thanks in the cup of his blood. Yet the Christian is confident that the end of existence is not death but resurrection and so his "yes" perdures. It is the song of such a "yes" that the new morality sings.

For all that has been "thanks."
For all that will be "yes."

REV. DAVID P. O'NEILL

Forming Christian Consciences

Some Practical Guidelines for Parents and Teachers

A group of Catholic parents in one corner of our parish decided that they wanted to know their priests and one another better, and so they gathered—usually around ten of them—in one of their homes about once a month in the evening, inviting one of us along to join in their discussions and to answer questions. "Father, how do we go about forming a true Christian conscience in our children?" was the opening question put to me at one of these informal gatherings. The conversation brought out many of the questions parents and teachers are asking about forming consciences; in this article I am presenting the substance of it in the hope that it will be helpful to others.

I asked these parents what difficulties they encountered in helping the growth of conscience in their children. Whey they had warmed up a little, they overwhelmed me with examples and problems. One of the women mentioned a boy of eighteen, the son of a Catholic friend of hers; he was very scrupulous about sins, most of which seemed to be imaginary; he was going to confession several times a week, but it didn't seem to do him any good at all. "How can I make sure," she asked me, "that my little boys don't grow up like that?"

Another mother described the case of a seven-year-old boy who was having fearsome nightmares about going to hell; he had started bedwetting again, and refused to go to his parish school or to church. A child psychiatrist had advised his mother, among other things, to transfer him to a State school. "I know this is an extreme case, Father, but don't you think that there's something wrong with the way the Sisters fill the children's minds with ideas about sin and hell?"

This question prompted one of the fathers to tell about his daughter, aged seven, who asked him what impurity was. When he questioned her, he found out that "impurity" was one of a list of mortal sins she had to memorize before making her first confession. "I don't think she's capable of mortal sin," he concluded, "and I don't think she needs to know anything about it for years yet."

So it went on. The parents' worries were mainly concerned with the kind of legalistic approach to morality which they felt their children were absorbing through their religious training in the schools. (In New Zealand, parochial schools are not supported by the State, but almost every Catholic child attends one.) The Christian life was apparently being presented to them, in its main emphasis, as a matter of not doing a certain number of things, which must be carefully learned about; if you did any of these things, you must tell it in confession so you could go to holy communion. Some of the parents were quite vehement in criticizing this approach, others felt that while criticism of the schools was quite justifiable, they themselves were as much to blame as the teachers in insisting on so many "don'ts" in order to preserve good order and polite manners in their homes.

One of the fathers, a schoolteacher, defended the Sisters and Brothers. "How would any of you parents," he asked the rest of them, "like to keep order in a group of forty children for five hours a day, five days a week? A teacher is forced to concentrate a good deal on prohibitions, and spend a lot of time dealing with petty offenses. It's no wonder that when the religion period comes around, the Sisters slant their teaching on morality the same way. This is one of the reasons why I think that formal religious teaching shouldn't take place in school at all; it should be done with a very much smaller group of children than you get in a school classroom. Perhaps we're expecting the Sisters to do the impossible, trying to train forty or so Christian consciences at a time. I don't think you can do it that way. At all events, Father must have a good idea by now of what our difficulties are; let's ask him what he thinks about them."

Conscience, I told them, is the final stage of a very slow growth in a child's powers of self-knowledge and self-control; its existence is not very evident before the middle years of childhood, and it certainly doesn't finish its growth before late adolesence. In fact, it should go on developing throughout adult life. It is quite unreal, then, to think that when a child comes to the "age of reason" about the age of seven, he can be presumed to have a fully-formed conscience.

The Basis for the Development of Conscience

The earliest growth of self-control, with the accompanying feelings of self-satisfaction, shame, and guilt, begins in that mysterious area of babyhood and early childhood beyond the range of conscious memory. Psychologists think, however, that this growth springs from the love-security relationship of the child with its mother and father, and from their efforts to train the child in acceptable ways of habit and behavior. This is why psychologists pay so much attention to how early toilet and cleanliness training are carried out, and to temper tantrums, and why they emphasize that such matters must be handled in an atmosphere of love and security, with a warm-hearted tolerance free from false adult attitudes of disgust and shame. In all early disciplining, the child needs to experience loving acceptance as a person, for this is the ground out of which his own idea of himself and his powers of self-control will grow.

All parents are familiar with the stage of development at which a small child begins to show a "guilty look" when he feels that he has done something that they will not approve of. But this sense of "guilt" is not conscience as we normally understand the word—the rational judgment of our mind on the rightness and wrongness of our behavior. People who have trained young puppies will have noticed that they can show the same kind of guilty look about their misdemeanors. All such manifestations, then, are still on the level of instinctive feeling and reaction.

A good deal of the confusion between modern clinical psychology, which owes so much to Freud and his theories, and more traditional ways of understanding human nature, lies in a lack of appreciation of this distinction between what we call conscience, and the instinctive feelings of guilt or self-approval summed up under Freud's term "superego." He describes the unconscious process of identification by which the small child absorbs into his own mental and emotional structure the demands, standards and cultural traditions of its parents. This process develops a kind of self-control in the child, attempting to limit and channel his deep-seated urges and drives so as to fit in with parental standards. But this controlling force can become tormentingly intense when the child is in great dread of losing altogether the love of its parents as he understands them. (This is one reason why all small children need the daily, almost hourly, assurance of being loved by their mother and father.)

We have only to think of our own feelings of guilt and shame to realize that they do not always correspond to the rational judgment of our conscience; how often we find our real conscience arguing with our instinctive feeling about something we have done! How common it is to find people deeply anxious to confess some fault which they know intellectually to be trivial or nonexistent. For example, many people will confess that they missed Sunday Mass, although they had valid reasons for doing so. The psychologists further analyze many more levels and functions of self-control and self-judgment. But, above all, it is important for parents to understand this primary and basic distinction between the level of instinctive feeling and that of rational judgment. If they do not differentiate these clearly, they will not easily realize the vital importance of their tolerant loving of their child in his earliest years. For it is out of the child's appreciation of the love of his mother and father, a love which is warm, secure, unlosable, that his natural power of self-criticism, self-judgment and self-control will gradually grow. And if teachers are to share in promoting this growth, it can only be by providing in the school, in spite of the problem of numbers, a similar atmosphere of love.

This need is well summed-up by Leon J. Saul, in his book *Emotional Maturity* (Philadelphia: L. J. Lippincot, 1947.) "Even adults learn best from teachers of whom they are fond; and, in the last analysis, the child accepts the restrictions of life and the standards imposed on it, provided these are within normal limits, through the fact that it loves and is loved; but if it feels that it is not loved and is trained, for example, only by domination, then its incentive to accept standards is gone; it learns only through fear of punishment and is apt to develop hatred and rebellion not only towards external authority but also towards its inner representative of these, namely, its own conscience. Moreover, hating authorities, the child cannot identify with them, and so lacks adults upon whom to model itself in its struggle towards emotional maturity."

The Growth of a Conscious Response to Love and to Objective Values

I covered this ground in a conversational way with my group of parents and summed up by stressing (1) that it is from the relationship of love and from the identification of the child with its parents that self-control naturally develops, and (2) that it will develop well only within an atmosphere of constant, secure loving, since conscience will only grow truly as a loving response to love received.

One of the fathers then remarked, "Father, I can see you mean that a lot of our complaints about school should really be directed against ourselves rather than the teacher. But how about all this insistence on sin with the seven-year-olds in our schools? Can a child really commit sin at that stage?"

I told them that I didn't have any final and clear answer to this question. Up to about the age of seven, it seems fairly clear, the child sees right and wrong only instinctively, in relation to its parents' demands and standards. When this development of inner control is good and true, the child will, at about this age, begin to make a response of love to the love he senses in his parents. He will give evidence, at least occasionally, of a loving obedience which is more than a well-trained instinctive response, no longer coming from a fear of consequence, but from a true appreciation of love in the person of the parent. This is the point, in good and normal development, which indicates the first growth of what we call conscience, a true self-control, in conscious decision, growing out of the feeling-control at the instinctive level. Many people think that this stage is usually reached around the age of six to eight years.

At this stage also, a child begins to see parental demands and standards objectively, to recognize them in the world of reality which he is beginning to sense outside the arms of the parents and the walls of his home. He begins to realize that actions can seem right and wrong in themselves, not only for him but for other children, and even for grown-ups.

Parents should encourage this development when they begin to see it. They should let the child see that they, too, are bound by these objective standards of right and wrong in dealing with others. They should let him see this in their own dealings with him, and not be afraid to apologize to him if they feel they have been hasty or unjust with him. They must treat him fully as a human person with all the rights and dignities of human persons, so much talked of today. Thus through the experience of being treated humanly, of being the subject of reverence and honesty, the child will grow in a sense of his own human dignity and of the reverence, respect and honesty he must show to others.

But for healthy growth, obviously, the child needs gradually to find a harmony and unity between these dawning objective standards and the early-child "instinctive" standards absorbed from the parents' love, behavior and demands. When such harmony is lacking, his whole growth is stunted and retarded, and the seeds of conflict and anxiety strike fertile root.

The child's self-control, then, grows out of his love-identification with the mother and father and his absorption of their standards into his own internal system. Later, he begins to see that these standards have some objective meaning in the wider world of outside reality, that there are things which are, in themselves, right and wrong. But there remains a further step to take, and a very big one, before a child can commit sin.

The Development of a Christian Conscience— Response to an Awareness of God's Love

Sin implies a conscious relationship to God in our behavior; we say that it is "a deliberate offense against God." When the Christian child is taught to pray and to grasp the simple facts of the Gospel message at an early age, his understanding and sense of God is closely merged with his love-identification (or lack of it) with mother and father. Only in the love of his parents can he begin to see the meaning of God. He learns of God as Father; as a loving obedient Son born of a human mother; as the love of Father and Son, their personal Spirit of unity. He learns gradually that beyond the love of his mother and father there is the further reality of God, of the Spirit of Love in Father and Son. He senses this deeper reality as the model of love, received and honored even by his own mother and father.

The child's early powers of self-control and initial conscience are a response to the loving care and standards of the parents. As a child begins to sense an even deeper reality and energy of loving care in God, he experiences a similar demand of personal response, since love always demands love in return. This call of God's love in the heart of the child gives an added dimension to the child's power of self-judgment and self-control; it opens the way to the active holiness of the Christian life, and to the possibility of committing sin. Until this added dimension grows into clear focus, a child is incapable of committing sin.

So we find three dimensions in the development of conscience. The first, developed in very early childhood, is at the level of instinctive feeling and reaction; perhaps it grows originally from the child's instinctive fear of being separated from the love and secure warmth of the parents, which leads him gradually to internalize and make part of himself their demands, standards and training. The second dimension develops as the child begins to see objective reality in his standards of self-judgment; this is the beginning of what we call conscience, operating at the conscious level of his understanding of human values. The third dimension is that of holiness and sin, as the child begins to appreciate God as the center of love, from which all love and law derives; he hears God's call of love to his heart, and feels within himself a demand for love in response. It is the deliberate rejection of this call, the retreat from this demand, which is the essence of sin.

When Does a Child Become Capable of Committing Sin?

The group of parents went on to discuss what I had said in relation to their experiences with their children. Most of them thought that the things that their grade-school children had been taught to call sin were really only naughtiness at the natural level of behavior, and did not really involve the children in any deliberate rejection of God, even in a small way. They all agreed that a real consciousness of sin would come at a different age for each child.

I commented that it seems very difficult to suggest any general age at which sin becomes a normal possibility. One traditional view has held that this happens about the age of seven, a view still reflected in the custom of having children begin to go to confession at about this age. However, psychologists who have studied the religious development of children are more and more inclined to doubt the possibility of sin at this stage in the child's development. They doubt whether the average child of this age has a sufficiently clear appreciation of God and his love to feel personally the connection between this love and his own unruly behavior. Moreover, they also doubt whether the child's powers of deliberation are sufficiently developed for him to be able, at the moment of yielding to his instinctive urges to misbehave, to make the conscious choice of right and wrong required for the theological notion of sin.

In the present state of our knowledge of the religious psychology of children, we may probably conclude that we must look to a later stage of development, perhaps about the years eight to twelve, for the time when a child is capable of deliberate, conscious sin. It does seem that not until these middle years of childhood is the young Christian capable of fully conscious decision of commitment to God's love, a commitment sufficiently liberated from his early-child instinctive attitudes to his parents and teachers to be considered fully his own as an individual person. And it is therefore at this same stage that formal sin, a deliberate and fully personal retreat from the will of God's love, could become a practical possibility.

I agreed with what the parents had said that this development cannot be fixed at any given age for all children; it will differ with every child according to his own speed of psychological growth, and according to the type of response he has come to make to the kind of family upbringing and early schooling he has received.

"So really," I concluded, "we can't fix any age at which a child becomes capable of committing sin. It would seem as though the average age would certainly be later than seven years. But the only one who can attempt to decide about an individual child is someone who knows his personality and behavior very well and who also has his confidence, someone who will listen to him and bring to light, not just his memorized catechism answers about God, but his own deeply personal feelings and attitudes about God's love and his own behavior."

One of the mothers remarked that what I had just said was quite a comfort to her. She referred to her eight-year-old daughter, and the difficulties of taking her to confession. "She never seems to be able to think of any sins to tell in confession, and it usually ends up with one of us suggesting things for her to tell the priest. We've felt for some time that she really hasn't caught on to the idea of confession at all. But I can understand now that maybe she hasn't been committing any sins yet; her conscience doesn't accuse her of anything before God. I suppose the only thing for us to do is to try to understand her real self, as Father said."

The schoolteacher in the group then reminded us of what he had urged earlier in the evening—that we were expecting the impossible of Sisters when we expected them to train and form the consciences of a whole classroom of children at once. He was now more convinced than ever that this was a work for parents; it is they who should decide, after talking it over with the priest and the teacher, just when the child should begin to go to confession. Both the Sisters and I, I added, would be very happy to have parents undertake this responsibility. I also said, in answer to another question, that to have one of their children receive holy communion regularly before making a first confession would present no difficulty.

What about Mortal Sin?

The schoolteacher then reminded me that I hadn't dealt with his question about mortal sin; he asked me at what stage the normal child could be capable of mortal sin. "In the first place," I told them, "I think most people underrate the difference between venial and mortal sin. St. Thomas Aquinas said that it was like the difference between being sick and being dead." We see this difference best when we look at the Christian life as a relationship of love between God and ourselves, as the living, active response of our whole being to the love of the Spirit living within us. "Mortal sin" means that we totally and deliberately break off this love-relationship—we deliberately and knowingly choose to do something so largely and gravely against God that it involves a complete change in the direction of our living, a turning away from love. Venial sin, either because the wrong action concerned is more trifling, or because there is less knowledge or deliberation, does not involve our whole self in its turning away from love; it leaves our essential commitment of love intact. The difference between venial and mortal sin is, therefore, like the difference between the ordinary quarrelling of husband and wife, and a total breaking-off of love, with separation and divorce; or like the difference between the common angry scene between a teenage boy and his father, and the kind of final quarrel when the boy packs his bags and leaves home for good.

A great deal of confusion about mortal sin is caused by the lists of mortal sins provided by theologians for catechisms and prayer books. These lists are meant, surely enough, to be helpful; to indicate to us that these actions, such as neglecting Sunday Mass, have about them that large quality of evil, of wrongful self-centeredness, that, when done with knowledge and deliberation, they may be mortal sins. Unfortunately, many children memorize these sins and learn from doing so that it's a mortal sin to miss Mass on Sundays, to do something impure, etc., without ever realizing that the essence of a mortal sin is a deliberate breaking-off with God. They feel that every time they do one of these things it must be a mortal sin, regardless of whether or not they have deliberately turned away from God. The net result is that many Catholics, after years of Catholic schooling, can remember lists of mortal sins, but don't really know what a mortal sin is.

In this light, look at mortal sin from the viewpoint of a child, remembering the kind of maturity necessary for this total rejection of the love of the Spirit, this deliberate turning away from God. We can be quite sure, from all that the psychologists tell us about the child's slow growth in the appreciation of objective values and in his powers of active deliberation, that this kind of deeply significant and totally involving action is not at all possible for a seven-year-old, or even a ten-year-old. This practical certainty is reinforced by our common sense view of the relatively minor significance that we give to the apparently serious doings of our children. When a ten-year-old girl says to her father, "I hate you, and I'll never speak to you again!" he generally considers it to be merely a bit of bad temper. When even a twelve-year-old boy announces that he's had the whole family in a big way and is going off to live on his own, the family still expect to see him at the next meal.

Thus the kind of serious psychological involvement necessary for mortal sin does not seem possible before the beginning of adolescence. Even then, when counseling the young adolescent, we must be very careful in estimating his responsibility for his rebellions to take fully into account the natural disturbance of urges, drives, and emotions which go along with his confused striving for independence.

Once again, the answer to the question about the age which a child can commit mortal sin, can be given only for each individual case. It can be given only by someone who knows the child well and understands his present stage of development sympathetically. Even then he will very generally not be sure. In fact, the more a priest learns about mortal sin and studies child development and religious psychology, the more hesitant he becomes of his own judgment of a child's conscience, and the more he realizes that the only true judge is God.

Stressing the Development of Love

We can see now why we speak of our conscience as the voice of God within us. Every detail of a Christian's life, to the extent to which he is committed to the love of the Spirit within him, comes under the self-judgment of love; it is part of his total response to love. A Christian's life with God should be something like that of a young man and woman deeply in love with one another—the whole fabric of their lives in every detail becomes a part of their dedication to the love of the other. In this sense, the conscience of a Christian becomes the voice of the Spirit of Jesus who, by the totality of his loving, becomes the model of our living. St. Paul refers to his conscience being enlightened by the Holy Spirit (Rom. 9, 1); the dark corners of our mind need the light of total love to see the way to the Father, Jesus himself, who said "I am the Way."

At this point in our meeting, the parents began to discuss a number of practical consequences they had drawn from what I had been saying; that the whole of moral education should be a training in love under the guidance of the Holy Spirit; that parents and teachers should always be making sure they are not obscuring or obstructing this work of love in the child's soul; that the Church's teaching about hell can have no meaning except terror for a child until he is old enough to understand personally something about mortal sin, since mortal sin is a tentative beginning of hell on earth; that they should never attempt to frighten children into goodness by false threats about God not loving them when they are bad, since children need the same total security of love at the spiritual level that they need at the natural level of family life.

From these last thoughts, the mother who was worried about her eighteen-year-old friend suffering from obsessive scruples eventually came back to her original remark. "I still want to be very sure, Father, that my boys don't grow up with that kind of conscience. All that has been said here tonight will be a help, of course, but is there anything more that we can do?"

"Help your children to grow in love for other people and for God," I said. The case she had mentioned—by no means an isolated one—highlights the importance both of parents' understanding more about their role in developing their children's consciences in an atmosphere of real love, and the importance of teaching about sin only in relation to love. This case shows what can happen when a young man's conscience has not developed beyond the infantile stage, and when it is wholly directed by fear. But a young man of eighteen with a rightly developed conscience should be entering into full maturity in the Christian life. He should have a strong confidence of being liberated from evil by the love of Christ. His conscience should be love-centered, realistic, responsible, with a firm community basis—that is, he should understand, at least to some extent, that his decisions for holiness or sin have a wide importance outside himself, for the whole of the body of Christ, for the whole race of men. A young man's conscience, at this age, is a reflection of his whole psychological development, of his whole maturing as a man; it is out of this natural structure that the high Christian life of love must grow.

As I went on to say, we must not separate our Christian faith and living into two parts, doctrine and morals, for it is all one. We see this very clearly in the Masses of the great feast-days: the revealing of our new relationships of love with the Father, the Son and the Spirit is the energizing source of our new life of holiness; what God reveals to us and does for us (doctrine) is equally the revelation of what he asks and enables us to do in return (morals). In the Christmas mystery of the Son's common nature with us we find that we, too, are royal sons of the Father, ransomed from all our guilt; we must then, be a people set apart, ambitious of noble deeds. In the paschal mystery, we find that we, too, have risen with Christ, sharing in his victory over evil and sin; so we cannot escape the demand to lead a new life in the risen Christ. In the mystery of Pentecost we find that the coming of the Spirit to the apostles is equally a coming to our own hearts, where he dwells in love; we find that we must live as people in love, people whose every thought and action comes under the rule and judgment of love.

This is the simple, direct view of Christian commitment which parents and teachers must constantly be opening out to a child. As each great truth and its corresponding challenge takes deeper root in the child's life, it brings with it its own light for his conscience and its own firm confidence of self-judgment, as he enters more and more into the strong security of the love of Father, Son and Spirit.

But the child will find little meaning for his conscience in being a "son in the Son," filled with the Spirit, if the Christian message is negatived in practice by the teaching, in home or school, of a petty-minded anxious morality, giving the impression that the Christian life is a set of pious prohibitions designed for the avoidance of danger and damnation. Every child must be guided in the increasingly confident exercise, in the Spirit of love, of his God-given royalty of conscience. He must be led to see the laws of Scripture, of the Church, and, in due proportion, of his parents and teachers, as sure guidelines to help him find his own very personal answer of love. Perhaps the simplest way to say this is to suggest that children must be treated as persons. Instead of a brief, "Do this, or else"; or "Don't do that, it's wrong"; parents and teachers might say instead, "What do you feel you should do about this?" Or, "What do you feel about that—do you really think it would be right? Could you think of any other way of doing it?"

This does not mean, of course, that parents or teachers are expected to conduct a nondirective counseling session every time some order needs to be given. It does mean that their efforts should be along these lines in all the more important areas of conscience-building. Above all, they must remember that such urging to judge and decide should be applied not only in the negative areas involving avoiding danger of sin, but even more in the positive areas in which the child must find his way of making his own personal decisions for Christ under the power of the Spirit.

The parents by now were thinking of their baby-sitters. One of them volunteered as host for their next evening in a month's time. Another suggested that next time they should give me a rest and invite to their meeting two of the Sisters from the school to talk over all these matters of conscience-training with them. All agreed, and that is what they did. Perhaps this article will move other parents and teachers to do the same.

PAULETTE MARTIN

Teaching the Fall as a Stepping-Stone to the Redemption

As a teacher, and particularly as a CCD teacher, I find that one of the hardest things to do is to "think myself back" to the level of the children I teach, and to try to imagine what their reaction is to the teaching we present them with. Over the years there have been so many accommodations, sudden changes in perspective, new insights added to the little nucleus of a theology we started out with that it is hard to assess what kind of picture we are suddenly focusing on what was, in many cases, a fairly blank page. First impressions go so deep and they are often so hard to shake in favor of a broader picture, that it seems vital that we know just what that impression is.

The difficulty, of course, is that nothing is harder to get at! Children from seven to eleven, tremendous as their response is to anything new, are generally too wrapped up in their feelings to rise above them and "describe" them—or so, at least, we assume. Add to this the fact that in the past it was hardly the fashion to ask children for their reactions, or to encourage any critical awareness in them, and the further fact that there is a sacrosanct atmosphere about the teaching of religion, and it will hardly seem surprising that children have not come up spontaneously with their reactions.

Even at home, I have found, it takes a great deal of reassurance, delicate probing, and an atmosphere in which criticism seems natural, part of a general awareness that truth is complex and a challenge to get at, before children will admit to what they feel and think. We forget too easily that small children are dependent, and always a little fearful of grownup reactions.

With all these difficulties it would be easy to ignore the problem, and assume that all was well. It is only recently that we have begun soliciting reactions from teenagers. Why go beyond?

This was, I must admit, somewhat my own reaction, until I discovered that my seven-year-old son was not looking forward to his first communion, and that he would not admit as much to me but only to his older sister. After a few heart-to-heart talks all around, my ten-year-old daughter sat down and wrote what she thought, which I submit for its shock-value.

Lots of children don't know what sin really is. When they prepare their holy communion all they're thinking about is sins. When teachers try to show how kind God is, like the story of Adam and Eve, they also tell about the punishment, they tell a lot about the punishment. So, children think God was mean to punish them for such a little thing, at least they think it's a little thing. Also, they're scared of sin because they think God's coming down to hit them or something. They don't know God is coming to them in a spiritual way. They don't feel they love him. Lots of children are afraid to tell their parents, like my brother. When I made my holy communion I felt that God was in me and was giving me grace. That was because I had a good teacher. I didn't yet know about sin. When I went to another school I learned about sin. But now I felt differently about God. I felt that God was unfair and bossing people around.

There is nothing extraordinarily new about this confession. In fact I'm convinced it's the reflection of a general state of mind. But it is straight from a child's mouth, and as such, I think, worthy of thought. It should encourage us to ask a basic question which we are too ready to shy away from: it is the question Father Hofinger asks in his famous interview after the Eichstaett Conference:

What is the best order of presentation and what doctrines should be emphasized if catechesis is to be of greatest profit to people today, to develop and confirm a real Christian life in them and form faithful disciples of Christ who give witness to him? In presenting the whole kerygma, what should we emphasize? [1]

If the kerygma is above all the joyful message that we are called to sonship in Christ, then nothing must be allowed to obscure that joy. This is what the new catechesis aims to do, but we have thought too little about the "drastic rearrangement of doctrine" [2] which this may demand. The interesting thing about this child's reaction is that it shows that children are not really impressed by what we say about God: they judge him on the basis of his own words and actions. And the first action with which they are presented in the old catechisms is not one of salvation but of punishment, so that the whole context of God's plan appears negative from the start.

Creation, it is true, comes before the Fall, but the Creation story is far less vivid and striking than the story of the Fall: it seems to be setting the stage for the real dialogue between man and God which follows. The main thing children retain from this very

[1] Johannes Hofinger, S.J., *Imparting the Christian Message,* p. XI.
[2] *Ibid.,* p. XV.

dramatic confrontation is the unhappy ending: death, pain and the fact they have trouble learning their lessons (!) are all the fault of Adam and Eve, and in the back of the mind is the thought that it's also the fault of this all-powerful God for setting up this test in the first place. Isn't the urge to "know" irresistible, and who could hold out endlessly against curiosity? Behind this issue of "obedience" or "disobedience," children sense much more: adult evasions of their wish to "know" about life. The story reinforces their feeling that there are terrifying sanctions lurking in wait for those who ask forbidden questions, above all the ultimate religious questions of whether God is just or unjust, life meaningful or meaningless. It is safer to make a bow to authority rather than playing with Promethean fire. So the dominant lesson that children draw from the story of the Fall is one of religious conformism, and the main feeling they are left with is a vague uneasiness about a God who seems intent on keeping his creatures down to size. Children see their own situation mirrored in this part of Genesis; they inevitably—and rightly—identify with Adam and Eve, which is a measure of the genius of the storyteller. But any attempt to "justify" God with abstract definitions of original sin merely develops in them not a sense of sin but a sense of guilt, for the simple fact that they lack, at this age, any understanding of the objective evils of sin.

Catechists have become increasingly aware of children's reactions, and of the difficulties involved in presenting the story of the Fall "straight" from Genesis. On the surface the story appears dramatic and direct, certain to appeal to the childish mind. But it involves, as I hope I have made clear, not a naive but a very sophisticated view of man and nature and sin, which children are not prepared to understand.

In addition, the biblical renewal has made us aware of another problem besides the psychological one—the question of historicity. Children tend to believe that the conversations in paradise were overheard and taken down verbatim. When this idea has become anchored in their minds, it becomes very difficult for them to realize, later on, that Genesis was written by a Jewish author of about 1000 B.C. for an apologetic purpose—to explain how sickness, pain and death can exist in a world created by a God who is all Good, and that the only possible explanation lies in man's freedom to go against God's plan, to sin. The distinction between the truth of a theological parable and the "truth" of a historical chronicle is, again, something which small children are not equipped to grasp. For older children, who already have some sense of history, the difficulty can be resolved as some German catechisms have managed to: by presenting Abraham and the Promise, then going *backward* in Genesis to the Creation and Fall. This has the double advantage of establishing a difference between Abraham as a historical figure, and the inspired interpretation of myth, at the same time as it starts off the study of salvation history on a positive note. God's enveloping, even maternal love, which is so evident in the promises made to the patriarchs becomes the whole context.

Even for very small children, this sort of re-ordering might be possible. But eventually the question of how to present the Fall must come up, and here it seems necessary to re-consider what presuppositions conditioned the presentation of doctrine in the old catechisms, and whether they need still condition our own.

The key difference between the old and the new approaches lies in their view of redemption. The old catechesis saw the redemption mainly from a juridical standpoint, as the blood-payment for our collective sins. The offense to God's infinite majesty demanded an infinite payment, and none could pay this debt but his Son. In such a perspective, it is necessary to show first that the debt exists, which is the function of original sin. But this is a jurist's view, which by no means exhausts the riches of salvation, and in fact lends itself to easy distortions. First and most important, it arbitrarily separates God's mercy from his justice—and what a Moloch-like God it makes him appear, even if he exacts this payment from his Son in our stead! In an effort to compensate, to bring out the reality of God's love, great stress was laid on the crucifixion, but this mainly succeeded in dissociating the Father from the Son, he who punishes from him who suffers.

And so the liturgical spirit, which rests on admiration and wonder, was impossible; people were thrown back on private devotions. Perhaps worst of all, the theological picture which this view of redemption left in the mind was one which amputated the kerygma of a great part of its meaning: the resurrection and the second coming were slighted because the incarnation was not seen as a way of raising man to sonship, of imparting to him the divine life through union with Christ, the head. If our Lord was the second Adam, he was merely thought of as having re-established the *status quo* of before the Fall, as having "satisfied for our sins"; "heaven" in the popular mind was confused with "paradise." Grace was seen as something exterior, a cloak thrown over our naked souls, an almost mechanical application of Christ's merits to ourselves, and the Holy Spirit who proceeds from the Father and the Son was pretty generally left out.

Perhaps I have somewhat darkened the picture to make my case. The liturgy was always there to amplify the picture for anyone who chose to look to it, for example in the prayer from the Mass which says:

O God, who established the nature of man in wondrous dignity, and still more admirably restored it, grant that through the mystery of this water and wine we may be made partakers of his Divinity, who condescended to become partaker of our humanity, Jesus Christ your Son, our Lord.

But it is this insight on the incarnation, and the view of the redemption which this prayer reflects that the catechetical renewal is trying to recover today. The "kerygmatic approach" is above all a recovery of the whole kerygma, stressing the *joyful* content of the message that we are raised to sonship. In Father Hofinger's own words, it is "incorporating the conclusions of the biblical and liturgical movements." But what are these conclusions? How can we incorporate them without attempting to define them? Shouldn't the reordering of our presentation of doctrine begin with a broader and deeper view of the "core" of revelation which these movements have brought us?

The enormity of the job is almost discouraging. The task of assimilating so many rich insights in our catechesis is barely begun, but it seems to me that one place to start would be with some new definitions of the redemption which would be more inclusive than the old ones. If the new catechesis is to reflect the liturgical spirit, it must first of all give a view of God's plan of salvation that will fill the beholder with admiration, and anything which is not consistent with this aim must be struck out. We must find a view of the Fall and the redemption which will exalt God and fill children with a sense of worship, which is precisely what the old presentation failed to do.

One way to do this, I believe, would be to stress a view of the redemption based on freedom. If the underlying design of salvation history is God's persistent wooing of his creature's love, his gradual raising of natural man to the perfect love and freedom of a Son, then all of his actions—the creation, fall, incarnation and redemption—must be seen in the light of that purpose. They must be interpreted from the standpoint of Christ, in whom all things stand revealed. In the past, we have often felt that to exalt God we must debase man. But the very essence of the Christian message is that God is Love, and his greatest mystery that he seeks to exalt his creature to himself. Then his greatest gift to man is freedom: the freedom to love or to refuse love, to cooperate in his plan or to go against it, to sin. Man's disobedience in the Fall is the necessary first act in a drama which reveals God's glory because it proves the value he gives to man's freedom. That freedom is not illusory, since God is willing to consent even to the ruin of his creation for the sake of that free act of love he hopes to elicit from his creature. Truly, he has made man "in his own image and likeness" since he gives him the chance to say "I will not serve." Then all the subsequent acts in the drama acquire the more meaning from the way God sets about salvaging his creation without in the least violating man's freedom.

It may be protested that this is beyond the grasp of children. But if there is one thing that all children understand, it is the fact that no one can force them to love. If there is one thing they respond to, it is respect for that freedom, and once they are convinced that they are being treated as persons they are willing to respect that freedom in others. This is precisely what they respond to in the personality of our Lord, and they must be made to see from the start that he reflects the will of the Father. Only when we can present the Fall to them in this positive light should we present it at all. For only then can they have a truly filial attitude toward God. Only then can they see what concerns them most: suffering, death and injustice, not as reflecting God's will but the denial of his will, not in the light of "punishment" but as the real effects of the mis-use of our freedom.

This underlying design of freedom also illuminates the incarnation. What infinite ingenuity inspired God to find this way for man to participate himself in his salvation, and the creation of the new heavens and new earth of which St. Paul speaks. No one had more insight into this design of freedom than St. Paul. We must communicate something of his own admiration of God's plan for winning our love without in the least forcing it, for transforming pain and evil without abolishing them arbitrarily, so that we might be able to win our salvation and not simply have it thrust upon us. For as we cannot doubt Christ's love, because of his humanity and his acceptance of all the conditions of human existence including utter shame and failure, so we are drawn to love him too, and through this love which is already the Holy Spirit within us, we are united to him, the new Adam, and enabled to share in his transfiguration. What greater respect for our dignity would be possible? How much more there is here than the payment of a debt, the satisfaction offered to God's justice! There is the possibility of our offering him an act of worship in keeping with what we receive, which is the whole meaning of the sacrifice of the Mass. Here is the perfection of love that does not humiliate the receiver but exalts him into the position of a giver.

So Christ does not so much "buy us a ticket to heaven" as graft us onto himself, the true vine, so that the kingdom of heaven begins to grow in us here and now. The sacraments are not mechanical channels of grace so much as encounters with the risen Lord whose own life, the life of God himself, springs up like a fountain of living waters within us, but we must be really present to meet him here. United to him, the head, we will necessarily be united to one another. Just as the original unity of man in Adam was broken by the turning away from God, and Genesis is a record of the consequences of that disunity, so man will be knit up again to unity in Christ. But only insofar as he wills it, for man is to be a creator along with God.

Presented this way, such a "theology of freedom" is very abstract and admittedly unassimilable for children of almost any age. It can only be presented implicitly through Scripture, where God's word and action are one, as Father Hofinger has made clear. But our own understanding of the design, our own preconceptions will color our presentation and will determine what comes through. What we leave out may at times be more important than what we put in, for as God has timed his revelation in accordance with man's understanding, it is important that we imitate his realism.

But there should be one guiding principle throughout: that the God we present should be consistently the God of love as our Lord knew him, and that we never be obliged to take back, at a later stage, what we said earlier. There will always be a need for some definitions, so it is necessary for us to see clearly where some of the definitions of the older catechisms were too narrow and left no room for growth, and to have the courage to throw them out—even if we have nothing, immediately, with which to replace them. Above all, we must be wary of too simplified definitions of the redemption, which is the heart of the Christian message. We must be aware of the way in which all of the Old Testament narrative has been made to fit in with a legalistic, moralistic conception of the atonement—which some of the new books, for instance, are making an effort to re-define as at-one-ment.

And no doubt, the most determining factor of all will be whether, as teachers, we have a real respect for the persons we teach, no matter how small, and faith in the Holy Spirit to do the real work. For if we try to quench their critical awareness or to force a superficial adherence to either Christ or the Church, we are undermining the very message with which we have been entrusted and giving our children a stone in place of bread.

SISTER FRANCES MARY MYERS, S.L.

Teaching the Meaning of Sin and Salvation

"Catechetics for the Real World" is the title given to a recent article by Brother Gabriel Moran, F.S.C., in which he states, "The upheaval to come in catechetical development may be far greater than most religious educators envision." This writer agrees wholeheartedly and maintains that the upheaval should begin immediately in the elementary grades. This is not to deny that a great updating of the quality of religious instruction has already taken place in many of our parochial and CCD schools, but anyone in the field knows that an urgent need still exists for the upheaval of which Brother Moran speaks.

The doctrine of original sin, Adam and Eve, the garden, and the whole mystery of salvation come immediately to mind as the area where teachers in the grade school could begin. Most religion teachers are eager to comply with Pope Paul's assertion of last July to a group of theologians and scientists gathered in Rome to discuss this very subject:

> Your purpose is to put into relief the present state of exegesis and of Catholic theology regarding the dogma of original sin, with special reference to the findings of modern natural sciences, such as anthropology and paleontology. The fruit of your comparative research should be a definition and presentation of original sin that is more modern and that better satisfies the demands of faith and of reason that modern men feel and manifest.

It is my hope in this article to develop for elementary teachers one approach to a more modern presentation of original sin and, hence, to a more positive presentation of the mystery of salvation. The development here will be directed mainly toward junior high level but can very well be adapted to intermediate and primary grades.

Let me begin by stating my belief that the first eleven chapters of Genesis should not be used with small children. The literal interpretation which a child is bound to give these stories makes an impression which is most difficult to dispel, and this literal interpretation, no doubt, accounts for the negative notion of salvation held by the majority of our young people today: "Jesus came to open the gates of heaven which were closed by the sin of Adam and Eve; Jesus died on the cross to save us from our sins; our first parents caused all the suffering and evil in the world and that is why we have to go to school." These and others like them are the standard answers given by most students in our religion classes today.

A child's early years should be given over to discovering and experiencing what it means to be loved by God, thereby awakening in him the desire to respond to this love. During this period, children should be helped to find the beauty and wonder of the world around them. Much time and thought should be given to ways of bringing children to a growing realization of the wealth of knowledge, enjoyment and self-development which comes through the eyes, ears and other sensory organs. During these awakening years, parents and teachers must stress the goodness, mercy, and love of God who has made all these wonders possible. Thus, a deep respect for life and the privilege of possessing human life will begin to take hold of the child. Recently, a first grade teacher asked her students what they say to Jesus when he comes to them in holy communion. One typical answer: "Dear God, thank you for everything. I hope we will be good to everyone. We are happy that we can come closer and closer to you. We are happy that we are persons and not rocks, trees or flowers. These are beautiful, but we are more beautiful because when you come close to us we become like you."

The *Word and Worship Series,* a recent publication of Benziger Brothers, with both a Catholic school and a CCD edition; and "Discover," the new primary material in the *Witness* series put out by Geo. A. Pflaum, Publisher, will be of great assistance here; "Joy," a new publication of *Mine* magazine, also uses much the same approach. All these materials focus on the immediate life experience of the child and help him discover God's presence in and through them. They aim to aid the teacher and the parent (all have parent editions) to confront the child with questions about life which he can see, hear, touch, taste and smell.

Only after this sense of values and attitudes has been firmly rooted, only after the child has an intense appreciation of his worth and his potential and has developed this same appreciation for others, should any mention of sin be introduced, because sin can then be seen as a rejecting of all these realities. Sin will be understood as being their own personal failures and the failures of others to love and to help others (and oneself) live fully, and this understanding prepares the way for the notion of solidarity in sin or "the sin of the world" referred to by St. John, which we enter into at birth.

I suggest that teachers begin, so far as their own thinking is concerned, with the definition of original sin offered by Father Hulsbosch in his book, *God in Creation and Evolution:* [1] "The powerlessness arising from nature, of man in his uncompleteness as creature to reach his freedom and to realize the desire to see God, insofar as this impotence is put into the context of a sinful world."

Obviously, no elementary teacher is going to state this definition in so many words, but it will serve as the framework within which to develop what is being referred to by many theologians as the dynamic approach to original sin. It would be worth every teacher's time to read the treatment given this approach by Reverend Peter de Rosa in his new book, *Christ and Original Sin.*[2] It is probably one of the most helpful references to date dealing with the subject.

Children of any age can be helped to realize that the first and most immediate need for salvation lies within themselves. The teacher might open up the discussion by asking a few pertinent questions: "Have you ever felt jealousy when your classmates received an honor or prize?" "Do you get angry when your younger brothers or sisters are given privileges which you were not allowed at their age?" "Do you wish you were more popular or better looking?" Questions like these open the way for discussion, and soon the students will begin to talk about their weaknesses and limitations. Recent happenings in the classroom and playground could be used to advantage. Encourage

[1] Ansfried Hulsbosch, O.F.A., *God in Creation and Evolution* (New York: Sheed and Ward, 1966), $4.95.

[2] Peter de Rosa, *Christ and Original Sin* (Milwaukee: Bruce, 1967), $3.95.

Or, if we say that "the trinity" acted to save us, such a statement is equally unfaithful to the New Testament deliverance, as it comes to us.

The catechetical problem, it would seem, is how these words, these ideograms—"God," "Son," and "Spirit"—stand for the three greatest Realities in human life, which is one Reality.

One keeps thinking of John Wesley and June Star. They are eight and ten at the moment, and they are driving to Florida. Will those three words stand for the reality of love that enters into their lives by the time they die, or will they merely live out their lives as Christians and get Christian burial?

All of us know some genuinely committed Christians who have been made such by God's action through the Church. But we need to worry about the obstacles we have set in the way, or what is wrong with our work that it doesn't happen often enough. We are right in assuming there is no flaw in the work of the Holy Spirit. Why do we not let him form Christians in the image of God's Son more often?

We who are catechists know that we have the problem of analogy. We know that God can only be taken in by us by way of symbol. We cannot know him as the infinite, the absolute. We would have to be the infinite and the absolute to know him as he is. So we use the symbols with which he has provided us, such as our faith and the language of faith. They stand for God with sufficient accuracy so that we may really believe in him and not in the symbols.

Tillich's solution is a radical one. He says that we can know something of the very ground of our being—that which underlies our existence—the absolute, only through giving answer to his unconditional demands.

Who is God? He is that one who underlies all my life—the lives of all men within the compass of that universe which is other than he. He is the one who sustains and supports us, and we come to know him through giving answer to his unconditional demands.

Bultmann would say that Jesus is the one who put the least conditions on his response. He was authentically himself because he took seriously and without reservation all the moral and political choices he was faced with, and most especially the challenge of the cross. Tillich would say of Jesus that he looked within to the creative ground and meaning of all our existence, and he was ultimately concerned over it. Bonhoefer speaks of God as "the beyond in midst of our life." Kierkegaard refers to a "deeper immersion in existence."

Is this line of thought "immanentism?" Do we simply dismiss it by tacking a label on it? There is, in fact, nowhere to go except to the depths of one's own consciousness to know God. We cannot flee to any other place—if you will excuse the spatial metaphor in a Bultmannian context. We can only know him as through looking within (assuming the necessity of first taking in the world through the senses). In the depths of our being we discover him through use of the right symbols such as "Father" and "Son." "Philip, he who has seen me has seen the Father." These ideograms are taken out of human reality. There are fathers and sons only in human families. The words are sufficiently helpful to give us some clue to the divine reality. We come to this reality only in the depths of our consciousness.

Is God personal? We have always answered "Yes" to that, we Christians. We have been saying lately, with intensity of conviction, "He is above all personal," and "The Christian does not 'know' God unless he is in an intimate, personal relation with him." God is personal, Tillich would say, in the sense that ultimate reality underlies all that we experience as personal. "God is love" (John's phrase) means that in pure personal relationship we encounter the deepest truth about reality. God is the one who gives himself most fully without hope of return. This being so, only the man who has loved can say what God is.

The definition of God, we said above, is "the self-given," by which is meant in the first place the interiorly self-given, as among Father, Son and Spirit. But in this latter sense, it may reasonably be asked, "Who cares?" We care because God is the self-given to us as well. If you have loved you can know him whose definition is that he is love. If you have not loved you can never know this by being told that he is love. What is specifically Christian about our view of the world is that we assert that *the final definition of the reality of personal relationship is the love of God in Christ Jesus our Lord.*

Now, how is all this our problem? The catechist is someone who must know the great realities. God must be real to him. However, God's personality is, as Rudolph Otto suggests, the visible, conceptualizable "one-tenth of an iceberg" that shows. The rest, the other nine-tenths, is the numinous that we take in non-rationally.

I do not wish to be parroting, merely, the ideas of deep thinkers. I do wish to say I think that many of these ideas are right. If we teach God as a person (I mean God the Father) as if we could understand him fully in his personality, the eight-year-old child will know that this is not true. He senses immediately that

God is much more mysterious than that—and the catechist has lost the eight-year-old child. God our Father is chiefly incomprehensible mystery to us, with a little bit of what we call "personality" showing. Christ is the sacrament of God. He is one in whose presence his fellows felt inadequate—dust and ashes. "Depart from me, I am a sinful man O Lord," said Peter (Lk. 5, 8). Christ is definable personality, as we know it, in a way that his Father is not—though during his lifetime his Father *was* such a definable personality to him. We do not suppose for a moment, however, that the Father of Jesus Christ can be Father to us in exactly the same way as he was Father to him. The Spirit is that breath or force or power that makes men love—that is responsible for superhuman realities in the midst of men. Do men do a thing which is beyond their powers? It is the Spirit who is responsible for it. He is person from the very fact that his divine power underlies all that persons do that is quite beyond themselves.

The catechist, in knowing those three great realities, Father, Son, and Spirit as they can be known, will necessarily know them through the signs which stand for them best. He must know those experiences that evoke the reality of God's action in men's midst most effectively. Which are the experiences that evoke the reality of God's action best? They are chiefly sacramental experiences soaked in charity, and after that, all other experiences of love than the sacramental ones. I mean to designate as the best signs of the three persons in God human inter-personal love-relations: experiences had both with the aid of sacramental signs and apart from sacramental signs.

We have said that the catechist must know those words which interpret best the meaning of God's action in men's midst. Now those words are chiefly, but not exclusively, the words of Scripture. Often biblical speech is conceptual; but sometimes it is not. Sometimes the spoken or heard interpretation of what God is doing now or has done in the past is by way of conceptual interpretation; but more often it is not. This is not to say that the testimony to God's word comprised by the Bible has no idea content. Obviously it does. I am thinking for the moment, of the Isaian Apocalypse (Chapters 24-27), or a little snatch out of St. John's Book of Apocalypse such as 21, 1-7, or the entire fourth gospel where the reality of God's action is interpreted to us verbally but non-rationally as much as rationally. Speaking in tongues, as done in the early Church and occasionally today, is a manifestation of God's action.

The catechist must use interpersonal relations for what they are. They are the clearest sign and best analogy for the saving work of God among men. We feel at times, unquestionably, that we must write off words such as "lambs," "shepherds," and "good seed." "Father" is of no help at all in situations where young people despise that word upon hearing it because of the reality it stands for in their lives. The same is true of "son" for the girl of nine who knows she should have been a boy. She learned it five years before, and by now the notion of sonship is hateful in her ears. We do, in fact, therefore, write off certain words as being of little help in conveying the great realities, knowing that we have to find better ones to convey the realities they stand for. But the reality in every situation is the relation of love among persons. That is what is signified, whether by the sheep-shepherd image which says love to some people; by the father-son image which speaks tender concern to many although not to all. What is the reality behind all these symbols? It is the charity that enlarges, the charity that frees, the charity that is solicitous, the charity that heals.

For the Christian there is no such thing as "mere humanism." It was quite shocking to hear a certain Council father refer to Schema 13, in debates on it during the third session, as "too humanistic." I think that is impossible: to be "too humanistic." None of a Christian's humanism is mere humanism—the Christian who understands his faith, that is. We consult the needs of each other's manhood, and in so doing we discover God. Our loves with which we love are divine loves. We have been told that in faith. We must expand them and explore them so as to find them.

What, in fact, do we do? We have a genius for choosing signs that smother, signs that lead away from the God within. Even when we have the right signs, such as the sacraments, we tend to do the wrong things with them.

There is another story in *3 by Flannery O'Connor* called "A Temple of the Holy Ghost." In it a girl of twelve is being visited by two older girls of fourteen; the two older ones go to a circus, a country circus in the south, and at a sideshow they see a hermaphrodite. The little girl wants to know what they saw. She bargains with them: "I saw rabbits born once and I'll tell you how they are born if you tell me what you saw at the sideshow." Then they explain how the freak, as he is called, walks on either side of a curtain lifting his dress to the people on each side and saying a mournful tone, "I'm going to show you this and if you laugh, may God strike you the same say. . . . This is the way he wanted me to be and I ain't disputing his way. . . . I'm making the best of it. I don't dispute hit."

The little girl has learned from the week-end visitors who went to the circus that in their convent school they have been described by a Sister who teaches them as "temples of the Holy Ghost." This is what they should tell boys who get fresh in the back of a car, the Sister says: "I am a temple of the Holy Ghost." The little girl who has been told the story of the freak says, in keeping her part of the bargain, that the mother rabbit spit the baby rabbits out of its mouth. That night, lying in bed, she tries to work the whole thing out. How can a freak like that be a temple of the Holy Ghost? In this case the child has discovered a real life problem. It is right for her to have it. She also has a fitting sign, the person's strange body and tortured mind. God's love is indubitably manifest somehow in this poor creature who is making his (her?) living this way.

At the end of the story they go back to the convent school where the two are deposited on a Sunday afternoon. In three minutes, at the very close of the story, the child is smothered in various important signs of Christian faith which are used wrongly in this instance. As soon as they come to the door they are bundled off to the chapel where benediction is in progress, by a Sister who meets them at the door. I need not tell what the smothering signs are. Well-worn hymn tunes, the air heavy with incense, the monstrance held aloft, the Host shining out ivory-colored in the center. The mystery of the eucharistic body of Christ is totally concerned with the way in which the

Spirit-filled risen Jesus becomes a means to make us temples of the Holy Ghost. This sign has never said anything remotely like that to the child. One has the feeling it never will. And all the time the little girl is thinking of the tent at the fair that had the freak in it. The freak was saying, "I don't dispute hit. This is the way he wanted me to be" (pp. 191-93, *passim*).

Putting the case of the relation of sign to ultimate reality another way, we might refer to the film *Becket*. There is a scene in it in which the King of France is discovered by his friend Becket in a compromised position with a young woman. The king is in a self-defensive but by no means embarrassed position. Becket is already showing signs of religiousness, and so the king says to him: "You can have your world, I'll have mine."

Now in some way this is the catechist's problem. Half the world has a cosmos under its palm: an immediate, easy-to-interpret sign of ultimate reality, whatever that reality may be. At first the sign is thought to stand for pleasure without pain: the pleasure of a human relation without its responsibility. The sign stands immediately for the urge to creativeness, the urge to be fruitful. But more basically the "world" under the palm is a sign of an interpersonal relation, for now the man is accepted by another and he accepts her. Even though we say that the terms of the relation are bad, it is its power as an anodyne that recommends it. A man can endure a lot in virtue of those intervals in which Eve is seen as the garden—the paradise of pleasure.

The chief problem of religious formation is that of helping men to regulate their love lives. They need to put *eros* in the service of *agape,* or if that verbal figure of submission is bad, relate *eros* and *agape* as they must be related. In a word, religious formation consists in providing an experience of human love which will be divine love. This will necessarily be the case if it is experienced by Christians in the way that Christians love. It will be human love transcended, transformed.

The right signs will be made to stand for the right realities, the ultimate ones, in the minds of those who are catechized.

CATHERINE B. KENNEDY

Forming the Relevant Community

An Experimental Senior High School Program

Within catechetical circles today, ways are constantly being sought out to make Christianity relevant to the young people who come for instruction, whether it be in the formal religion class of the local high school or the once-a-week meeting of a CCD group. Teachers seek to develop within young people an awareness of their Christian responsibilities within the real world of everyday life and at the same time to provide a stimulus for faith. One major difficulty we encountered in Chicago was the fact that the senior year textbook in each of the major new high school religion series was still in the barest experimental form. Stimulated by discussion with committee members of Chicago's Religion Teachers' Association, the author, therefore, sought to gather materials which could be meaningfully used with seniors during this "interim" period. The concept of *community* seemed to be a unifying theme toward which the materials could be directed.

Articles from current periodicals were edited, significant excerpts cited, discussion questions formulated, and relevant paragraphs from Vatican II documents correlated with this overall theme. The end-product was an experimental text of approximately 200 pages.*

* Copies and further information may be obtained from Miss Catherine Kennedy, Apt. 6 C, 2661 Marion Avenue, Bronx, New York 10158.

These materials were mimeographed and individual copies given to approximately 1,000 students in five high schools in Chicago, to students and faculties from four CCD groups, and to faculties from several other secondary school religion departments. In most instances, the materials were handled in the "semi-non-directive" approach, alternated with smaller group-discussion sessions. Teachers and students attempted to face squarely the problem of commitment and to learn from the experience of community on the four levels of *home, school, parish,* and *world* the very real fact that only through faith and living "in Christ" can one hope to carry out his Christian commitment.

Student reaction was spontaneous and highly receptive. They wanted their religion to be meaningful, to relate to their daily lives; the framework of a discussion-orientated class, they felt, gave substance to this desire for relevance. They requested more articles on: (1) the role of the teenage laity in the Church today; (2) woman's role in the Church; (3) poverty and the Church; (4) lay institutes; (5) God's place in the family; (6) love; and (7) maturity. Some articles they felt were "too intellectual" and abstract. Greater use of audio-visual materials and film-discussions was suggested, but they vetoed most discussions on dating and sex, as well as on the "open generation." Encouraged by the young people's response, I hope through this article to share the general course content with other teachers facing the same problems and to stimulate further dialogue on the religion curriculum for both CCD and the Catholic high school.

The *approach* used in the course is threefold. An introduction to the needs, influences and challenges of each community structure is followed by several articles from current periodicals, edited for the students' notes, and read prior to class; a clarification of terms contained in the required readings is followed by a discussion of the role which this particular community plays in the development of faith. With this common background to work on, group or general discussions, structured by question-guides accompanying related quotations, take up several class periods. After each student has formulated a response to the matter in question, teacher and students together search out the mind of the Church; that is, what God is telling us through Scripture, his vicars, or Vatican II. This latter discussion brings out the fact that a complete, authoritative answer is by no means provided to every problem and challenge in life. One finds very often that the answer lies within the heart and soul of each man, or that there is no *one* answer.

Assignments are geared to the section of the material being discussed: i.e., reading of other related articles not included in the notes—particularly, those appearing in the latest periodicals available in each classroom; the reading and paraphrasing of Scripture and Church documents in modern terms and examples; searching out illustrations from everyday life which make concrete so many of the more abstract discussions.

The *content* of the course of study follows an outline structured about the four communities of home, school, parish and world. Briefly this outline includes:

I. The meaning and challenge of the *Christian vocation* in the world today which demands a living, dynamic response in faith to the person of Jesus Christ and to his mission;

II. The concept of *community* is then discussed and defined as that framework wherein each person lives out his commitment of faith;

III. Now, the particular communities are studied with emphasis placed first on the world community as the place where *faith is challenged and lived.* The characteristics of this community are discussed, and particular areas are brought to the fore through articles chosen to stimulate thought. These areas are grouped under three headings: Christian "Absenteeism," Christian "Involvement," and Problems of Our Age which affect all forms of our community life. Absenteeism leads to a discussion of the political sphere, civil rights and racism, labor relations, and the communications media. Involvement stresses the lay apostolate, lay institutes, religious ecumenism, religious tolerance and liberty, freedom and authority. The problems affecting all forms of community life are seen as: the search for peace, poverty, drug addiction and alcoholism, population explosion, delinquency, and the use of leisure time.

The mind of the Church concerning these issues is then sought out through a study of selected passages from the Pauline epistles, the writings of John, Acts, and the Council documents on the Church, on the Laity, on Religious Liberty, on the Church in the Modern World, and on Ecumenism.

IV. The *parish community* provides the groundwork for study of the foundations of faith. Within the definition of the parish community, stress is laid on the priesthood of the laity which finds its fulfillment within this community. The relation of pastor to his people, together with Catholic action and the earlier mentioned "communities of interested Christians," stresses the transition to be made from the classroom community to the level of parish. Integrally bound up with the concept of parish is the role of the parish in the city. All too often, the relationship is one of divorce rather than of mutual support and concern. Because of the very definite dependence of the parish on the structure of the family, these discussions lead to consideration of the next major community—that of the home.

V. The *home community* is viewed as the place of *faith's formation.* For here the child encounters his first real definition of Christianity; else, he goes without an adequate concept of its relevance. The role of the home in religious education is discussed, and its central role in God's plan is emphasized. The Christian home is defined and the broken home also viewed. Here, a discussion both of the role of the modern Catholic woman and of the role and the use of sex, as well as its abuse, are stressed.

VI. The last community to be studied is that of the *school, where faith is constantly in transition.* It may appear to be misplaced—yet it is meant to carry out this precise role of transition. The student vocation is studied with particular relation to the vocation of the public school student. His searching out of his place in God's plan brings out his need to be a true witness to the fact that God still does act in our world through people and events. His witness role and his honesty with self and with others in his student vocation should testify to the fact that he is a Christian. Here, the issue of the pro's and con's of Catholic education, with the ideas of "legislated holiness," "sense of community," and "crisis in faith" are discussed as time permits. The last topic within this community centers on the role of the Catholic college, the witness sign on the secular campus, apostasy on the campus, academic freedom, and the place of Newman work in student life.

VII. In conclusion, life in community is viewed as being lived out in faith—a faith which is a response in love to the person of Jesus Christ and the effort to assume his attitudes ("the ability to think the thoughts of Christ") in all our relations.

The following materials, for example, are used in the unit on Ecumenism (in the study of the world community). The student first reads the following condensed and mimeographed articles: "What You Can Do for Christian Unity" by Douglas J. Roche in *The Sign*, November, 1963 (an interview with Father Gregory Baum, O.S.A.); "Parable for Renewal," an editorial in *Ave Maria*, July 17, 1965. The class then forms small discussion groups, and each choses its own "religion." They then work together to prepare a report on this religion according to likenesses and differences with Catholicism in six areas: scripture, liturgy, doctrine, organization, prayer life, and trends to unity. Questions to guide their reports include:

(1) What is the historical basis of the religion which you have chosen to discuss?

(2) What is your religion's definition of "unity?"

(3) How do you define the ecumenical movement within this Church?

(4) What are its liturgical similarities (or influence, if a non-Christian religion) to Catholicism?

(5) What is this religion's outlook on the place, role, and function of scripture?

(6) What likenesses and differences occur in major doctrines?

(7) Are there prayers for Church unity which are recited publicly or privately by this Church, and what is the overall sentiment they express?

(8) What plan of action would you suggest to move Christian religions toward reunion?

Suggested follow-up projects are: (1) Interview a non-Catholic friend and get his or her opinion on the subject of Christian unity. (2) What bibliography can you suggest for the study of this religion? and what source material was the background for your answers to the above questions? (3) If you have contact with a Protestant minister, a rabbi, or a priest, get his opinions on the idea of unity and invite him to come and give a short talk to the discussion groups.

The presentation of the discussion reports is followed by further discussion based on a series of excerpts and questions such as the following:

Sharing tables. Protestants, Catholics and Jews disagree . . . about the dogma of the Assumption, but we do not disagree about the dogma that every man is made in the image of God and that the color of his skin is therefore irrelevant in determining where he is entitled to live. . . . Right now, we can sit at the mayor's office table, sharing a common concern for fair housing, even though we cannot yet all sit together at the Lord's table, sharing a common meal. . . . What we learn of one another from our contacts at the one table may drive us to greater shame about our divisions at the other table and thus force us into deeper levels of confrontation than we have hitherto managed to attain (Robert McAfee Brown at Loyola, Chicago, excerpted from *Ave Maria*).

(1) What is the significance of the fact that we do not disagree on the equality of all men and the fact that each is made in the image of God?

(2) List some of the things which "we learn of one another from our contacts at the one table" (the table of conference in sociological areas).

(3) In what way does the following statement complement that of Dr. Brown? "(The Eucharist should be) interpreted and experienced as a sign of unity, since the Lord has invited all to his banquet to partake of one bread. . . . Its sad tragedy is that we have separate tables" (Cardinal Gracias of Bombay, quoted in *Ave Maria*).

(4) Why do all Christians desire to share the "Bread of Life" at a common table? What particular symbolism is there in the concept of "sharing tables"?

(5) Name some areas of confrontation which we should seek out in our dealings with other Christians.

These discussions are followed by the reading of a 7-page condensed version of the *Decree on Ecumenism*, with a final discussion geared to thinking with the Church in the present day as it seeks for unity.

The goals of such a course obviously involve ideals which cannot be measured. Whether or not these goals are achieved in the student's life ultimately rests with the personal, free choice of the individual for or against Christ. The course did seem to bring home to the students the fact that this choice is one's own, that times of such choice are truly the often talked-about "crisis in faith," but that they are also challenges to a deeper, more committed way of living the Christian vocation.

SISTER M. LORETTA KOLEY, R.S.M.
SISTER JEAN FREDERICK, R.S.M.
MARY DWORAK

Studying the Person in His Relationships

An Experimental Senior Religion Program

If anyone knows that there is a "Crisis in Catechetics—into the real world," it is the high school religion teacher himself. Brother Gabriel Moran, F.S.C., decries "narrowly conceived catechetical material"[1] which, in current catechetical revolutions, has replaced the old catechism but has not led instructors to "sink their teeth into the solid theology that is now available." We should like to present a program which might qualify for what Brother Gabriel describes as "a brief plan within which each teacher can use his own initiative." We feel that it can make the "subtle and indirect appeal" that is missing in "up-to-date and scientific" textbooks. The syllabus which follows is structured on current theology—a theology which rises from and is grounded in all the theological thinking of the past.

We believe it is essential that a religion program for high school juniors and seniors be so flexibly structured that it can develop easily along with developing theological thought. A textbook, of its very nature, is

[1] "Crisis in Catechetics—Into the Real World," Brother Gabriel Moran, F.S.C., *The National Catholic Reporter* (Kansas City, Mo.: April 13, 1966), p. 6.

obsolete almost before its publication. After the students in the freshman and sophomore years have been solidly grounded in Scripture and liturgy, teachers must face the task of providing a flexible, rather than a rigid, program. But flexibility is not sufficient. The course needs flexibility within a constant, that is, its theme and basic structure should remain relatively permanent while the specific materials used to develop the theme undergo constant replacement.

In trying to correct the inadequacies of a textbook, religious instructors are being swept into the opposite extreme: presenting current theological materials in a totally unstructured, haphazard and arbitrary fashion. We feel that it is essential that current materials be incorporated into one unifying theme—a theme which strictly governs the selection and rejection of materials and determines the emphasis which selected materials will receive. This theme should lead the student through progressive, sequential thought to one overall and vital concept.

The concept upon which the following syllabus for Mercy High School senior religion students was developed is that "All life is meeting" (Martin Buber), that life requires participation and not isolation.

Much of the vital quality of this program came from the joint participation of lay men and women, Sisters, and priests. In May, 1965, at the suggestion of Father Henry Schorn, CCD director of the Omaha Archdiocese, and encouraged by Archdiocesan School Superintendent Monsignor R. C. Ulrich, a group of lay and religious persons assembled for the purpose of drafting a syllabus for a senior high school marriage course. Marriage courses in existence seemed to have bypassed the relevant contribution which married laymen could make.

With the early appointment of Mr. Jerald Maiers [2] as chairman, the committee began collaborating with the teachers at Mercy High School, because the syllabus which these teachers were in the process of developing seemed to coincide with the general structure envisioned by the committee. The lay committee studied the materials, supplied professional speakers, and visited the classrooms themselves to relate their personal experiences as married couples. (These activities are described more adequately in the program which follows.) A writing committee consisting of two married couples, a priest, and a Sister [3] then prepared a greatly expanded program suitable for use during the 1966-67 school year, the one outlined here. The syllabus which follows, then, represents only a first attempt at a program based on flexibility within a constant.

In using the syllabus at Mercy High School, we made enough copies of all the articles for each student. We hope in time to have a materials committee

[2] Mr. Jerald Maiers: M.A. in Theology from Marquette University; Theology Instructor, Creighton University, Omaha, Nebraska.

[3] Mr. Jerald Maiers (identified above); Rev. Gerald Burbach: M.A., Diocesan Director of associated Cana groups and the Christian Family Movement; Mrs. Maryanne Maiers: B.A. in Speech Therapy from Marquette University; Mr. Gerald Hug: B.A. in Psychology (January, 1967) from the University of Omaha, Nebraska; Mrs. Ann Hug: B.A. in Sociology from Duchesne College of the Sacred Heart, Omaha, Nebraska; Sister Mary Marice Koley, R.S.M.: M.A. in Theology (summer, 1967) from the University of Notre Dame. Also, Mr. and Mrs. Carl Lyons, Mr. and Mrs. Terry Macnamara, Mr. and Mrs. Robert Meehan, Mr. and Mrs. Jack Sullivan, Dr. and Mrs. M. J. Wiltfong, and Sister Mary Teresanne Frederick, R.S.M.

responsible for making articles, tapes, and slides easily available to teachers, and we envision a wide enough selection of articles and other materials to make the program suitable for all-boy or co-ed situations as well as our own all-girl enrollment. We also intend to continue up-dating the materials.[4]

The program could certainly be adapted to CCD classes, but the adaptation would need to be very carefully thought out. We feel that the progression of ideas is very important and that it would be disastrous to pick and choose at random from the outline. There is also the danger that, when a class meets only once a week, questions raised without sufficient time to answer them would leave students more, rather than less, confused. But if a CCD teacher could count on the same group of students for two years, the program might be used as it stands. A thoroughly trained teacher should handle this problem.

[4] At the time of our going to press, hearings are being conducted in the House of Representatives on the revision of the copyright law which, it is hoped, will clarify the question of what constitutes "fair use" by educators of copyrighted materials. The established criteria are: "(1) the purpose and character of the use; (2) the nature of the copyrighted work; (3) the amount and substantiality of the portion used in relation to the copyrighted work as a whole; and (4) the effect of the use upon the potential market for or value of the copyrighted work." (See Report No. 2237, House of Representatives 89th Congress, 2nd Session, Oct. 2, 1966, to accompany H.R. 4347. From the Committee on the Judiciary.) But it is by no means easy to determine how these criteria should apply to the uses of various kinds of material in an experimental course such as is described here where a distribution of reproduced material far wider than to an individual class or school is envisioned. The freedom of educators to use such materials must be safeguarded (and many would argue with reason that such use helps to build up a future reading public for books and articles). But so, also, must the rights of the author, who must make a living from his writing if he is to continue to be useful to educators or anyone else.

Our first group of students had no special preparation; most of them had been in traditional religion courses for their first three years. They seemed to enjoy the course, tackled the difficult articles without any undue stress, and appeared to have learned from, as well as to have been changed by, what they heard, read and discussed. Their response seems to indicate that results do not depend on previous courses; however, we do not doubt that students would profit more if they were better prepared, especially in Scripture. At present, we are planning to give freshmen and sophomores such preparation by using one of the new texts. A junior course on the general theme of twentieth-century faith and morality is taking shape along the same lines as the senior course presented here.[5]

Although the three of us were teaching different sections, we tried to handle the same material at approximately the same time, with the result that students spent lunch hours and time before and after school discussing the material with their friends who were not necessarily in the same section. We teachers met frequently to share ideas and determine approximately how long we should take for an article or section. If one of us felt that she had spent sufficient time on a section and the other two wished to continue with it, the one who had finished arranged informal classes on topics of current interest or planned a class around questions posed by the students. The others then had an extra class or two to catch up. All of us were able at one time or another to hold such informal classes.

[5] For further information, contact Sister M. Loretta Koley, R.S.M., Mercy High School, 1501 S. 48th St., Omaha, Neb. 68106.

Overall Purpose

The aim of Mercy High School's senior religion program is to create in students an awareness that they can live more fully and vibrantly through interpersonal relationships than they can in isolation. It is based on the principle that growth in godliness requires growth in humanness and that this growth is usually a community and not an individual process. The philosophy of this program, then, is rooted in the historical event of the incarnation, which is the supreme instance of the human and the divine integrated into a single personality and of this personality forming historical community.

The teachers hope that students will come to view participation in its many forms as a vital opportunity in which the gift of self—that is, the act of self-expenditure—enriches the total community as well as, paradoxically, self. Christ himself, the grain of wheat which fell into the earth and lost itself so that it might not remain alone, is again the first instance of participation through self-giving. The content of discussion materials and the sequence of ideas in this program have been devised to help offset fear of involvement, with its risk of self-exposure, through showing that growth is primarily a mutual sharing of experiences. Since student relationships will be conditioned by a fundamental life situation, the program attempts to show the unique possibilities of "meeting" which marriage, religious life, and the single state provide.

The secondary, but ever subordinate, purpose of the program is to acquaint the students with the writings of men who have contributed eminently to the theological and anthropological ideas upon which this program is built. It is hoped that the books and periodicals which the students meet in this course will create such an understanding of and interest in religious ideas that they will want to undertake a continuing self-education through reading and thereby be ever able to interpret maturely their changing historical milieu.

UNIT I: *Building an authentic person*

Section A. Aim: To show through modern interpretations the misery of man in isolation and to suggest that authenticity of the "I" and genuine involvement with another, a "thou," are interdependent.

1. Alienation of man from man

a. "Eleanor Rigby"—45 rpm record by the Beatles. Paul McCartney composed "Eleanor Rigby" to protest the very loneliness that other communications media cultivate. The song, one of the top tunes of 1966, poses searching questions which the students will be facing throughout this introductory unit: All the lonely people, where do they all come from? where do they all belong?

b. Selections from *The Secular City* by Harvey Cox.

(1) "Playboy's Doctrine of Male"—pp. 199-204. The popularity of *Playboy* makes the message of Harvey Cox particularly relevant and interesting to high school seniors. *Playboy* presumes to solve the identity crisis of today's insecure youth by supplying a comprehensive and authoritative guide on how to be a man. Seeing that *Playboy's* philosophy ultimately exploits man's fear of total and permanent involvement makes it possible for students to discern similar anti-Christian philosophies in the mass media they encounter.

(2) "Cult of the Girl"—pp. 192-199. In this section of his book, Harvey Cox shows that young American girls can fail to be authentic because they regard the Miss America type of "ideal" girl as an idol. She functions as the source of value, the giver of personal identity, but spuriously, for only God can confer value and identity.

c. "Metamorphosis" by Frank Kafka (Part I), *The Best Short Stories of the Modern Age,* compiled by Douglas Angus, *Premier Book,* Fawcett World Library. Gregor, the principal character in "Metamorphosis" suffers from acute failure in self-awareness, self-acceptance, and self-realization; he *is* modern man in isolation, burdened by a sense of fear and anxiety, inflicted with guilt—not moral or theological or legal—but guilt arising from the failure to achieve real human personality and inward ties with his fellowmen.

d. "Theater of the Absurd" by Joseph Wilson, *Ave Maria,* January 22, 1966, pp. 5-10. "Theater of the Absurd," called by Martin Esslin, the "*true* theater of *our* time" forces its audience to face up to the truth of human life through experiencing vicariously the misery of man in isolation. In excerpts from works by Samuel Beckett, Ionesco, Genet, Pinter, and others, Mr. Wilson pinpoints loneliness as the theme of tragedy which underlies modern theatrical expression. "But," he says, "underlying the constant denigration of human circumstance is a rarely articulated theme which contradicts despair: it is the shadow of man searching, searching for meaning, searching for God."

2. Alienation of man from God

a. "God Is Dead"—Time, April 8, 1966, pp. 82-87 (deleted). *Time's* religion editors explore from almost every conceivable angle the question of whether the God-man relationship has changed and, if so, why. One explanation which the article suggests for man's religious anguish is the former identification of a biblical faith with Hellenic rational culture and the apparent cleavage of Christianity from life because of the present shift from rational culture to the existential. Besides making students aware of the secularizing process which has been continuous in western culture, the article introduces the idea that the secularizing process can be understood, not as an anti-religious force, but as the gradual growing of man into responsible adulthood, wherein he can relate maturely to God.

(1) Thomas Aquinas, *Summa Theologica,* Part I, Q. 2, Art. 3. St. Thomas' five proofs for the existence of God offer students an example of biblical faith identified with Hellenic culture. The highly rational argumentation of St. Thomas is basically Aristotelian. The teacher should point out the importance of a rational basis for faith, yet show the insufficiency of mere intellectual assent.

(2) Soren Kierkegaard, short, sentence-length selections from *Either/Or* and from *Concluding Unscientific Postscript.* The western world's shift from rational culture to the existential began with Soren Kierkegaard. In *Either/Or* and *Concluding Unscientific Postscript*, Kierkegaard shows that only through choice is authentic selfhood attained: life is a matter of either/or. Kierkegaard proposes a three-stage way to selfhood. In his development, the thinker may pass through the aesthetic stage (in which he experiments but does not commit himself), the ethical stage (in which he acts decisively and commits himself), to the religious stage (in which his sin is acknowledged and he commits himself to God).

Though his answer to how to become a Christian is overly individualistic and ignores the fact that deepest individuality is achieved within community, Kierkegaard fathered a respect for person which is at the root of many of today's social and religious upheavels.

(3) Friedrich Nietzsche, *Thus Spoke Zarathustra,* The Portable Nietzsche, edited by Walter Kaufman, Viking Press, 1954. "Zarathustra's Prologue"—pp. 121-4. To establish Nietzsche as the originator of the "God Is Dead" theory, students heard a tape recording

of the incident when Zarathustra comes down from his mountain to the world and, after conversing briefly with the hermit in the woods, asks himself what has become the modern query: Does he not know that God is dead?

First Part, 3, pp. 124-125. Students should be made aware of both the contribution and the error of Nietzsche. Nietzsche's overman is man bettering the human condition through attention to the world. Nietzsche's assuming that attention to the world is contrary to the divine will and therefore opposed to any belief in God is an instance of man's naive experience of God.

(4) Paul Tillich, "Great Radical Theologian—Apostle to the Skeptics," *Life*, November 5, 1965, pp. 40-41. John A. T. Robinson, *Honest to God*, pp. 44-49. Tillich succeeds where Nietzsche fails. Nietzsche sees opposition between God and the world; Tillich pushes through to the depths and center of reality where he sees God as the ground of being. The direction of religion, according to Tillich, is not to a God up and beyond, but to a God here deeply within.

Section B. Aim: To show that I-Thou relationships depend on the existence of an authentic "I" and to contribute to the student's development in self-awareness, self-acceptance, and self-realization. Students have seen man alienated from other men and from God. "Meeting" can provide the solution to this problem of alienation. Since "All life is meeting," students must realize that "meeting" others can occur only in the context of knowledge and love. The following program attempts to explore authentic knowing and loving.

1. Using a *real* object of beauty (e.g., long stem rose) the teacher introduces the students to the dual capacity they have to know things essentially and to know things existentially. Knowing the image "rose" is quite different from knowing the actual rose in bloom.

Once the difference is understood, students can begin to grasp the fact that both types of knowledge are necessary.

2. *The Decline of Pleasure* by Walter Kerr, Simon and Schuster, 1964, pp. 202-223 (greatly condensed). Pursuing the difference between essential and existential knowing, Mr. Kerr suggests that it is intuitive (existential) knowing in particular that enables man to grasp through actual encounter the mystery of unique person.

3. *Holiness Is Wholeness* by Josef Goldbrunner, University of Notre Dame Press, 1964, pp. 1-21 (greatly condensed). *Dialogues of Plato,* Washington Square Press. Short selections from Plato's *Republic* and *Phaedo. Republic,* ch. vii, p. 357-363 (abbreviated); *Phaedo,* pp. 77-80. The problem of essential versus existential knowing began primarily with Plato, who mistakenly attributed real existence only to essences. Plato's theory of existing ideas led to distrust of the world and bodily senses because they hindered the "ascent of the soul into the intellectual world."

The cave scene from the *Republic* graphically conveys Plato's dualistic theory of spirit versus matter. The dialogue between Simmias and Socrates in the *Phaedo* carries the dualistic theory through to its logical implications: The wise man will try "in every sort of way to dissever the soul from the communion of the body." Plato's theory, absorbed by Aristotle, made inroads into Christianity. Christians are just beginning to recognize the Platonic, rather than Christian, roots of many "ascetical" practices.

Father Goldbrunner sees sanctity as possible only on the condition that man abandon Plato's dualistic spiritualism. In the section cited above from *Holiness Is Wholeness* the student learns that authentic sanctity is founded on living one's own total truth; for sanctity is always bound up with authentic human life. Father Goldbrunner stresses the need for a person to trust himself to the inner workings of the intuitive mind and at the same time to allow the conscious mind to rise superior to and to exercise a decisive influence on the direction of the whole personality.

4. *Religion and Personality* by Adrian Van Kaam, Prentice Hall, 1964, pp. 43-51. This excerpt from *Religion and Personality* relates authentic personality to religious personality, self-experience with religious experience, and self-realization to a mysterious focus away from self and to participation in life. Father van Kaam points out that self-determination is a peculiar combination of freedom and obedience; he challenges the students to listen to and to stand out toward reality.

5. *Counselling* by Carl Rogers, "The Achievement of Insight," pp. 184-195. Failure to know and accept self plunged Barbara, a 16-year-old high school junior into despair and a nervous breakdown. In a series of counselling experiences, students watch Barbara grow into self-knowledge and self-acceptance. The real-life struggle described by Dr. Rogers invites students to identify with Barbara and to experience growth along with her.

6. A visit by a psychiatrist to discuss self-concepts and attitudes with the students should be incorporated into the program at this point.

7. *That Man Is You* by Louis Evely, Newman Press, 1965, pp. 49-50. This short selection from *That Man Is You* adds a personal and vivid dimension to the concepts of authenticity. In the person of David, the student sees the tragic consequences of man's suppressing self-knowledge. Through the judgment of Nathan, God reveals David to himself.

8. Christ called his followers to self-knowledge (Matt. 15:2-20 or Luke 6:39-45), self-acceptance (Luke 18:9-14 or 12:22-34) and self-realization (Matt. 25:14-30). His call, given in simple, sensory language to "whole" persons had little in common with ancient Greek dualism. Matthew's and Luke's gospels are filled with the

type of sensory images which establish Christ as an existential man. By the time students have searched out and savored some of the sensory images used by Christ, they are ready to study a summary chart that will graphically show the relation of Christ to Greek dualism and Thomistic theorizing. Christ's love was the love of a man who preferred persons to theories.

UNIT II: *Establishing a personal relationship with God*

Section A. Aim: To show the necessity of love in personal relationships and to show that love is the basis of God's relationship with man.

1. *The Art of Loving* by Erich Fromm, Harper and Row, 1956, pp. 25-32. Though modern man sees his problem as one of how-to-be-loved, Dr. Fromm shows that it is rather a problem of how-to-love. In this excerpt from his book, he defines love as giving and shows that care, responsibility, respect, and knowledge are a syndrome of factors necessarily present in persons who love. Seeing love as an art which can be studied and cultivated should help to offset common misconceptions of love as an unplanned and unpredictable feeling.

2. The book of *Osee*, chapters 1-3, *Old Testament.* If Dr. Fromm's qualities of love are correct, then these qualities will be evident in God's love for man. God's dealings with man described in Scripture, especially in the Old Testament, offer students a personal, heartwarming, and convincing exposition of love as giving, as care, responsibility, respect, and knowledge. In the tender and dramatic story of Osee and Gomer, God's love for man is revealed in human terms.

3. "Who Is Christ?" by Anthony Padovana, *Ave Maria,* February 4, 11, 18, 25, 1967: short, pertinent sections from each article in the series. In Christ man learns how limitless love can be, how tireless true love really is, how translucently brilliant a thing love can

be when it expresses itself even unto death and beyond hatred. Anthony Padovana's *Ave Maria* series, "Who Is Christ?" is a penetrating study of Christ whose ". . . appeal to love is so intensive that it continues even after our total rejection of him, beyond death, into Resurrection."

Section B. Aim: To show that God reveals and gives himself to us in Christ to be known as Father, Son and Spirit—in the biblical sense of the word "know," which includes love and union. *Theology and Sanity* by Frank Sheed, Sheed & Ward, 1946, pp. 74-83. Turning from a concentration on God's dealings with his creatures, Mr. Sheed explores God's own proper being and life and shows:

a. that God is truly a personal God who knows and loves;
b. that God experiences, too, his deepest individuality within community;
c. that knowledge and love are basic to divine relationships as they are to human relationships;
d. that total giving in love is always fruitful, benefiting the giver as well as the receiver;
e. that God expresses and reveals himself to us through his Son and that man knows and loves God through the Son incarnated in Christ;
f. that the mystery of the Trinity is not a contradiction in terms but a mystery of life and of love.

UNIT III: *Achieving conjugal relationship with another person*

Section A. Aim: To show that the nature of conjugal love demands a synthesis of all the powers of both persons: physical, psychological, religious.

1. Series of lecture-discussion classes on the physiology of sex given by Sister Mary Christelle Macaluso, R.S.M., Ph.D. College of Saint Mary, Omaha, Nebraska. In this section of the course, specialists in the

field of human anatomy should be brought in as guest lecturers in order to win the confidence of the students by speaking of their subject with professional objectivity and exactness. Slides, pictures, diagrams, and films are essential if the students are to gain adequate and accurate knowledge.

a. "Attitudes toward Sex." This first lecture-discussion attempts to create an atmosphere of frankness and objectivity in which positive attitudes toward sex can develop. The teacher attempts to free the concept of sexuality from the stigma of "concupiscence" with which it has so long been associated. Sexuality is presented as fundamental to human nature and as basic to human relationships.

b. "Male and Female Reproductive Systems." This instruction should give students a thorough education in the physiology of the male and female reproductive systems. The instruction should also provide the students with the correct terms for mature discussion of sexual relationships.

c. "Menstrual Cycles and Patterns of Rhythm." In order to interest and challenge the students, the explanation of menstrual cycles should be more thorough and technical than the usual "Walt Disney" approach. The students should be informed about the rhythm method of birth control and about contraceptive devices; they need to know the psychological, as well as physiological, effects of both methods. Moral implications can be mentioned here, but should be given more thorough study in the section on fecundity in marriage.

d. "Development of a Fetus." This lecture covers the important stages in fetal development and health factors important to both mother and child.

e. "The Birth of a Child." A movie on the birth of a child should be presented in which all the major steps in parturition are shown. This movie needs careful and thorough narration by a qualified person, preferably a doctor, who can answer student questions from his many experiences with patients.

2. "Marriage: the Lay Voice" by Michael Novak, *Commonweal,* February 14, 1964, pp. 587-590. Mr. Novak attempts to tell from a layman's experience that the problem of marriage is not that of abstinence and control but of response to another person. Mr. Novak stresses the integration of the physical and the psychic in this response, since he believes that the human psyche is so conditioned by maleness or femaleness that spirit and sexuality (in its broad sense) can never satisfactorily be separated. Mr. Novak also introduces some common misconceptions of sex—such as sex for sex's sake—that destroy part of the human response in an authentic love relationship.

•3. Psychological and emotional problems in adjustment to marriage. At this point, a doctor, preferably a psychiatrist or gynecologist, should visit the classroom to discuss psychological and emotional problems which arise in marriage.

4. "The Personality of Woman" by P. Parrain, *Marriage Is Holy,* H. Caffarel, ed., pp. 67-71. In Father Parrain's own words, this article purports to show how the personality of woman and the personality of man "complete and call forth one another." By stressing that the different but complementary aspects of man and woman are admirably realized in marriage yet "exist wherever men and women meet and collaborate in work and friendship as in love," the article challenges girls to begin now to develop solid, but femininc, personalities.

5. "My Husband Is a Great Lover" by Francis McGovern, *Marriage,* November, 1963, pp. 23-27. Students should be able to see in this love relationship the goal of mature love as described by Fromm, the mutual communication and response described by Novak, and the complementary aspects of the masculine and feminine personality described by Parrain. This article departs from theory and shows one couple's love and their ability to adjust to their particular life situation and to the personalities of each other.

6. Dating and Courtship. Young married couples—honest and frank, unafraid to expose themselves—can make the discussion of dating and courtship and early married life intensely interesting and relevant to the students. A brief introduction in which the couples give information about their dating and courtship experience is enough to prompt questions from the students. It is most important that the couples speak of personal experiences and avoid textbook answers to questions. Both husband and wife should be present at these discussions so that students can see the communication and honesty between them.

7. Canonical and Civic Aspects of Marriage. A survey of canonical and civil legislation should stress marriage as a contract, marriage as a sacrament, and marriage as a human and divine institution requiring unity and permanence. Separation and divorce cases could well be analyzed at this point of the course. A divorced person who understands the reasons why her marriage did not work out might make the students more aware of the need for mature judgment in the selection of a marriage partner and the need for unselfish attempts to solve problems as they arise in marriage.

8. The Council and Marriage. Article 48 of the *Pastoral Constitution on the Church in the Modern World*. Article 48 should reveal to the students the great care taken by the Council members to incorporate into their theological statements the findings of contemporary scientific and cultural research. The article shows that marriage demands mature interpersonal relationships and that personality and spiritual development are interdependent.

Section B. Aim: To show that conjugal relationship increases in dimension through fecundity in marriage.

1. Council Discussions about Marriage and Birth Control, *The Tablet,* November 5, 1964. Articles 49-52 of the *Pastoral Constitution on the Church in the Modern World.* Selections from *Casti canubii,* Pius XI. Selec-

tions from *Address to Midwives*, Pius XII. The discussion about fecundity in marriage which took place on the Council floor before the final drafting of the document on marriage gives the students some background for understanding the final document. The frank discussion among Bishops and Cardinals of diverse cultures and geographical areas led to a consensus among them that fecundity in marriage should be both generous and conscious and that judgment about how many children a couple should have belongs to the partners.

2. "Responsible Parenthood" by Bernard Häring, *Commonweal*, June 5, 1964, pp. 323-328. If man is, as Father Häring says he is, a being who expresses himself and knows himself only by listening to the Word of God and responding to that Word in love, then he can never support the ideas of the Planned Parenthood Association which encourages a single, fixed decision about family size, or resort to a legalistic approach which assumes that family limitation achieved through rhythm is always right. Both of these positions exclude personal response to the uniqueness of each situation and to the needs of love. God speaks to man anew in every circumstance of his life. If man fails to listen, he fails to live according to his nature, fails to be fully human, fails to participate in the universal law of growth. The Christian has no reason to regard the awakened consciousness about the engendering of new life as an undesirable development. A couple faced with the question of whether they may or should desire a new addition to their family should approach a solution through loving discussion. Christian prudence permits them to see all the factors in the proper light and proportion: Is the desire for another child here and now a true expression of love of God, of love of spouse, of love of children already born, of love of the being whose existence is really at issue? Prudence does not ask, once and for all: How many children do we want to have? Responsible parenthood is perma-

nently oriented towards the right moment as prepared by God, toward the present task.

3. Classroom discussions with couples on children and their effect on marriage. Most of the students are ready at this point to analyze their own position as children and to want to understand from a parent's point of view the challenge of rearing children in today's American society. It seems expedient that the couples who lead this discussion be parents of teenagers and be previously acquainted with the theological and anthropological principles upon which this course is built. Again, personal experience is the only source which will enable the students to identify themselves with the problems being discussed. Any deviation into generalized problems and answers typical of textbooks will alienate the students.

4. The Family. At this point a sociologist should be invited to visit the classes and discuss the family as a social institution. The speaker should touch on the major, traditional functions of the family unit and the forces which tend to alter these functions in an industrialized, urbanized, mobile community.

Section C. Aim: To show that Scripture expresses God's relationship with man as a nuptial union.

1. *Man and Wife in Scripture* by Pierre Grelot, Herder and Herder, 1965, pp. 85-118 (greatly condensed). In the last analysis any convictions which students have about marriage must find roots in the teachings of Christ himself. These few pages from Grelot's *Man and Wife in Scripture*, present students with the New Testament foundations for theological interpretations of marriage. Grelot shows that "the mystery of Christ which effects mankind's redemption is the mystery of a union in which God and mankind are face to face in the roles of bridegroom and bride." The nuptial mystery of Christ and the Church is not an otherworldly reality, completely beyond our grasp.

Grelot draws from Pauline texts to show that it is from our participation in it that the rules of conduct which govern our day to day existence spring.

UNIT IV: *Participating in the human community at large*

Section A. Aim: To show that a vocation to religious life or to the lay single life is a vocation of service to one's fellowmen.

1. Religious life. Because the religious state emphasizes universal Christian love, students should be led to consider its extension of the human personality to the needs of the community at large. Chastity, in particular, is the "vow of non-exclusive love" of all humanity. The "meetings" with humanity which religious life makes possible require, as Father Edward Hogan, C.Ss.P., says, an encounter, and openness on both sides by which persons "make each other be." Each religious vow, according to Adrian Van Kaam, C.Ss.P., is a listening to, an openness toward, and a love of all reality. A positive theology of religious life as a calling to participation rather than to withdrawal is an essential aspect of this section of the course.

2. "Christian Vocation to Love Given Direction in the Lay Single Life" based on a talk given by Mrs. Richard Edgerton, R.S.N. In spite of social pressures to the contrary, the lay single life can be one of fulfillment and of service. Only a mature adult, however, validly chooses to commit himself totally and permanently to the lay single state. Mature adulthood, according to Erickson's concept of growth and development, is the result of positive emotional growth through each stage of life. Satisfactorily solving conflicts which present themselves at various stages, the individual develops a sense of security, of autonomy, of initiative, of duty and accomplishment, of identity and self-awareness, and of intimacy based on mutual trust and respect. Man has really only one vocation: the Christian voca-

tion to love. To give direction to loving and a pattern for intimate relationships, the adult at some point makes a permanent commitment to married or unmarried life (lay single persons, religious, and celibate clergy). The lay single person chooses to work out his salvation as an individual through intimate relationships provided by his particular environment. He is in one of two positions: provisional, that is, as one who serves but is open to change; or permanent, one who for spiritual reasons and with the advice of a spiritual director makes a permanent commitment to the lay single life. This commitment necessarily demands that a certain age has been reached—minimum of late twenties—and that a definite apostolate is planned.

Section B. Aim: To show the ultimate unity of man with men and with God as expressed in the synthesis of Father Teilhard de Chardin.

1. "The Cosmic Piety of Teilhard de Chardin" by Rev. Robert E. Francoeur. *Catholic Mind*, December, 1964, pp. 5-15.

2. "A Fresh Look at Man" by Christopher F. Mooney, S.J. *Saturday Review*, February 26, 1966, pp. 21-24.

3. Very brief selections from *The Phenomenon of Man*, *The Divine Milieu*, and *The Future of Man* by Teilhard de Chardin, S.J., to clarify points of his theory. Teilhard's general theory is that "the whole history of the universe, life, and man has been that of a gradual ascent to greater complexity and consciousness, focused on and drawn by the Center of the Universe, Christ the Omega Point. It is an evolving process in which all things are centered on God and unite with Him" ("Cosmic Piety," p. 6). Matter, in Teilhard's view, is sacred and the universe possesses a sacramental character. Planning and shaping the world are of supreme importance to Teilhard and he reproves Christians for their apparent lack of interest in "grappling with the grimy machinery of society" and in identifying themselves with the city of man. Chris-

tians must do everything possible to promote and foster convergence—the coming together of society—so that individuals may achieve their fulfillment and full substance. "We have truly reached the parting of the ways: we cannot continue physically to exist (to act) without deciding here and now which of the two attitudes we shall adopt: that of defiance or that of faith in the unification of mankind" (*The Future of Man,* p. 255). Father Teilhard's theory that mankind is closing in upon itself in a relationship of love with Christ as the center makes a study of Teilhard de Chardin particularly suitable to conclude this course which emphasizes that "all life is meeting."

REV. DAVID P. O'NEILL

Can We Form Mature Christians?

"Christianity is a good religion for children, and even for adults who are still psychologically immature. That is why it is so popular—most people fail to mature completely, so they need a father-religion to give them security and protection. Human beings are children so long that most of them don't ever quite get over it. So Christianity answers very well to their deepest needs."

It was a very mature man who said this to me, a friend of mine who is a professor of sociology in a State university; a fine teacher, good research worker, warmly human and totally grown-up. I told him, of course, that what he said was very true, and he was encouraged to go on and explain.

"Think of the ideal Christian prayer, the 'Our Father'; an act of submission to the will of your Father, the King of creation, asking him for your daily food and for protection from harm. And Christ himself told you that you must become like little children again before you can enter your Father's kingdom. He summed it up beautifully in the story of the prodigal son; most people are basically insecure and lonely, afraid of their own evil and despair; they must have a father's arms to come home to. So they become the adopted children of God by the washing away of evil in baptism. They live anxiously; carefully obedient to their Father's laws in order to avoid punishment and to win his protection, love and final reward. As I said, this is fine for a great many people, but seems false for someone who is a mature and grown-up human being. Has he, after all his efforts, attained full maturity only to surrender it completely into the hands of God, so that he lives and acts only as an obedient child of a wise and loving Father?"

I told my professor friend that I would give him a low mark for his theology, but full marks for his social psychology. He had given a factual report, and a good analysis, of Christianity as he had heard it and seen it—in the lives of his students and friends, in many sermons, in much of its non-technical literature. Could we admit, too, that it was a fair summary of the kind of religion taught in many Catholic schools and Catholic homes? That even in practical Catholic life, a childlike submission to authority, and total unquestioning obedience are widely regarded as the supreme Christian virtues? In any case, my friend's attitude is that of millions of well-balanced, mature people in our Western societies; it presents itself as a crisis of faith for great numbers of young Catholics in universities; it may be a fair description of the meagre, immature faith of far more of us than we would like to admit.

So I told my friend that he began to go wrong in his theology at the beginning of the New Testament. The view he had of Christianity was a good picture of Old Testament Judaism with a few selected pieces of the New Testament fitted into it as a kind of enrichment of thought. But it was still unitarian, the religion of the one God. The whole message of the New Testament, of true Christianity, is in the one God's three Persons, Father, Son and Spirit. The Christian's commitment is to all three Persons, not to the Father only; his baptism is in the name of all three.

His view, I told him, was as wrongly incomplete,

as would be that of a psychologist who saw man only as an intellect, a thinking reed, without seeing him at the same time as a complex of drives, urges and emotions, all united in the physiological structure of the human body. Over-emphasis on any one of these three "components," to the practical exclusion of the other two, gives a distorted and false psychology.

What It Means To Be a Christian

We parted for the time by exchanging books—he to read the New Testament again, I to dig deeper into L. J. Saul's *Emotional Maturity,*[1] which I will refer to later in this article. Before, however, we look at what a modern psychologist understands by human maturity, let us look more closely at what it really means to be a Christian, to be baptized. The truth that marks us off as Christians is that when we are received by the Father as his children, and accept him as our Father, we also enter into an equally vital relationship with the Son and the Holy Spirit, a relationship of growth in love.

Those Christians who live by the limited view we have been considering, are something like the apostles before the Last Supper. Like the apostles, they are able to say the Our Father, to understand the direct message of the parables and miracles, to accept Jesus as their Messiah-Savior, to join in the procession of Palm Sunday. But they hesitate and stop before the full unfolding of the message that began on the Thursday night.

[1] Leon J. Saul, *Emotional Maturity, The Development and Dynamics of Personality,* (Philadelphia: J. B. Lippincott, 1960).

As we read St. John's account of the Supper, it seems that Jesus is like a teacher who realizes that his students are to face their final examinations the following day, and that so far they have made little progress in understanding what the course is all about. "All this time I have been with you," he comments sadly, "and still you do not know me." So, while knowing that they would desert and betray him, he speaks to them openly about the Father, the Spirit and himself.

Telling them about himself and about his intimate and permanent relationship with them in the future, Jesus uses symbols. His choice of common food and drink, the very necessities of life and growth, tells them, and us, that there must be constant maturing and growing-up in our relationship with him. He recasts this lesson in another picture when he tells us that he is the living vine grown by his Father, and that we are its branches and twigs, living by his life of love, the love he has received from his Father and is passing on to us. This love of his, and his joy which it brings to us, must grow to fill our hearts completely so that we will love one another with his own totally dedicated love, the love by which he lays down his life for his friends.

As if to reassure his apostles that their present understanding of all this, and their present love, are only a beginning of a new growth, he promises to send them his Spirit to be their friend and advocate in his place. We can understand, as they did not then, that this was yet another way of saying the same thing to them, for we recognize that the Spirit is the love in person of Father and Son. Jesus had already told them of the gift of the Spirit when he said, "I have bestowed my love upon you, just as my Father has bestowed his love upon me; live on, then, in my love." This spirit of love is equally the Spirit of Jesus and the Spirit of the Father, for he is their uniting bond of love given to us as a free gift, and as the source of energy of our growth.

Jesus promises his apostles that the Spirit will guide them into the full possession of the truth, the full understanding of the Father's message, which is Jesus himself. "He will bear witness," Jesus tells them, "of what I was." And, "He will not utter a message of his own . . . it is from me that he will derive what he makes plain to you. I say that he will derive from me what he makes plain to you, because all that belongs to the Father belongs to me." Finally, in the great prayer of dedication to the Father with which St. John ends this account of his, Jesus lifts us all up into the vibrant life of the Trinity: "I have revealed, and will reveal thy name to them, so that the love thou hast bestowed upon me may dwell in them, and I, too, may dwell in them."

The gift of the Spirit came to the apostles not only in the wind and flame of Pentecost, but also as a permanent memorial of love in what he inspired them to write. Particularly in the Epistles of St. Paul, we have the fulfillment for ourselves of the promise of Jesus that the Spirit would lead us into a deeper understanding of the truth about himself. St. Paul sees Christ as the new Adam, the leader of the new race of liberated men. Maturity, being fully grown-up, is the mark of this new manhood in Christ. His is the perfect manhood of full maturity; the previous growth of manhood is only childhood in comparison.

The task of the Christian, St. Paul tells us, is to grow up into the image of Christ, our elder brother (Rom. 8, 29). In the Epistle to the Ephesians, he tells us that it is through the gift of the Spirit reaching into our innermost being, that Christ finds his dwelling-place in our hearts, so that the whole of our lives are rooted in love (3, 16). He tells us that we must grow up into Christ: "So we shall reach perfect manhood, that maturity which is proportioned to the completed growth of Christ; we are no longer to be children . . . we are to follow the truth in a spirit of charity, and so grow up, in everything, into a due proportion with Christ, who is our head. On him all the body depends; it is organized and unified by each contact with the source which supplies it; and thus; each limb receiving the active power it needs, it achieves its natural growth, building itself up through charity" (4, 13-16).

When you read what St. Paul says, in the Epistle to the Galatians, about the way men lived under the Old Law in a spirit of anxious bondage like children under a tutor, and compare this with the view of the Christian life seen by the sociologist at the beginning of this article, you will understand why I told him that his theology was not Christianity. Lest any of us should go on teaching or living this distortion of the Christian message, we must listen to St. Paul telling us that "in those childish days of ours, we toiled away at the schoolroom tasks which the world gave us, till the appointed time came. Then God sent out his Son on a mission to us. He took birth from a woman, took birth as a subject of the law, so as to ransom those who were subject to the law, and made us sons by adoption. To prove that you are sons, God has sent the Spirit into your hearts, crying out Abba, Father. No longer, then, art thou a slave, thou art a son; and because thou art a son, thou hast by divine appointment, the son's right of inheritance."

"Sons in the Son"

Thus we are led back to re-examine our attitude to the Father. We find that it is only because he has sent his own spirit of love into our hearts that we are even able to call him Father. It is the personal love of the Son for the Father speaking in us, not any mere human anxious cry of a lonely child for its father's protection. While the human base of anxiety, loneliness, and awe remains part of us, it is swept up and enriched by the Spirit of Jesus dwelling in our innermost being, transforming us into sons of heaven, coheirs, true princes of the Father's kingdom. The Lord's Prayer, which, humanly viewed, seems to lead to the childish, immature view of religion, takes on a new maturity, a grown-up demand, when we join with Jesus in saying it, in his spirit of perfect love . . . "*Our* Father." This prayer is Christian only when we say it with Jesus, in his Spirit.

So, too, in the light of St. Paul's teaching, we see a new and deeper meaning in our Lord's command that we must become little children again. There is no other way into the kingdom save by accepting God as our Father; because Jesus is the Way, we must become, like him, sons totally dedicated to the Father in the Spirit of love. There is here no childish, immature dependence, but the free love of a grown-up son who is a royal prince of his Father's kingdom. Our way to the Father's love is no more childish than that of Jesus himself. It is the way of love without limit.

By the power and energy and fire of the perfect Love of the Trinity, then, we grow up in the form and image of the new and fully mature man, Christ; it only is in this love, in this new adulthood, by this way, that we come to the welcoming arms of our Father.

This whole effect of God's generosity and giving is evident in a child at baptism. The child is liberated from ancestral guilt, adopted by the Father as a son of heaven, formed into the image of Jesus, his elder brother, becomes, through the Spirit of Love, the sacred dwelling-place of the Trinity.

As the child grows, there must be a gradual acceptance of all that God gives him; there must be his own growing response of love to all the love and high dignity which he has received. It is only as he passes through the various stages of maturing as a human being, on the natural level, that he is able to make his full response to the gift and action of God within him. It is only as this happens that the dialogue of love between God and man comes to its full growth and fruitfulness.

So far is it from being true that Christianity is a religion only for children and immature adults, that it would be a much deeper objection to say that its ideals are far too high, that it is suitable only for very mature and well-formed people. This, indeed, is a much more difficult objection to answer. In view of all that we have seen of the true meaning of the Father's revelation in Jesus, how can we give the name of Christians to so many Catholics whose religion seems only a childish private distortion of the true message of divine love? If it is true that every neurosis has within it the elements of a private religion, can we wonder that Freud could view Christianity as a universal obsessional neurosis?

The Importance of Human Maturation

All of this points to the tremendous importance, for Christians, of their natural maturing as human beings. The whole process of human growth leading to the full development of personality should be the continuing basis of the formation and education of Catholics, in their homes, in their parishes, and in their schools. Without this basis of natural development, we cannot wonder that religious teaching does not take root in the lives of so many young people, that it takes only the shape of a private distortion; we cannot wonder that, as they grow into maturity, great numbers of them reject the infantile religious attitudes of their Catholic education.

When I re-read, in the light of this thinking, the book my friend had loaned me, Dr. L. J. Saul's *Emotional Maturity*, it struck me with renewed force that the full Christian life was impossible without the natural base of human growth which he describes. Saul analyzes eight major characteristics of emotional maturity, which are all closely interrelated and inter-acting. We might summarize his thinking, in non-technical language, under the three headings of ourselves, our relations with others, and our grasp of reality.

Maturity within ourselves demands a high degree of personal integration. There must be a well-integrated development of the various human drives and urges.

The forces of aggressiveness, hostility, and of sexuality must grow beyond the stages of child and adolescent development to the adult stage where they are at the service of the person for positive and creative ends. The inner forces of control must grow into the adult conscience which is not only a negative restraining force, but also a positive energy towards what is responsible and productive.

In regard to others, human maturity is marked by the gradual development, from infancy to adulthood, of emotional independence from the parents, to a point of grown-up self-reliance; there must be a growing sense of one's own value as a person, and a corresponding freedom from inferiority feelings, egotism, and undue competitiveness. All this leads to a mature capacity for warm and lasting inter-personal relationships, marked by the easy ability to receive and to give with equal grace.

A firm sense of reality, an emotional acceptance of the real world, is the final point of this summary. This grasp on reality will be marked by adaptability and flexibility of approach, and by freedom from various childhood fixations. It is through growth in these qualities that the adult is liberated from the unreal, day-dream worlds of fear, of hatred, of grandeur, of obsessive guilt, which create insecurity, inferiority, anxiety and loneliness.

In short, our mature man is well-integrated; he is responsible, warm and well-balanced; and he is realistic. The life of love demanded of the Christian in response to the gift of the Spirit is also summarized by Jesus in three forms: the love of ourselves, the love of those around us, and the love of God. Without the well-integrated growth of the natural self, there is no basis for proper self-love; without responsible, warm-hearted, and well-balanced emotional development towards others, there is no natural basis for the love of others in Christ; without a firm sense of reality and secure grasp of what is real, the basis is lacking for loving all that is real, in its center and source, which is God; without this deep aliveness to reality, one can hardly hear the voice of the Father in the message of Christ.

But God Is Love—Realistic Love

All of which brings us back to the very real difficulty that Christianity seems to be a religion suitable only for mature, well-balanced, realistic people—a corps of elite. The full Christian message seems to demand a response of love, of dedication, of self-perfection far beyond the capacity of the normal human being, handicapped as he usually is by all kinds of faults and deficiencies in his emotional development. As with our original difficulty, it is easy to appreciate the basis of realism in this argument. We have only to ask ourselves how many perfect Christians we have met—how many have we read about?

To take this argument to its final conclusion is to miss the meaning of love. A man and a woman in love, however mature they may be, however deep and secure their love, are not in love with an ideal human being, but with a real one. It is the realistic quality of their maturity which enables each to see in the other a real person, not a starry-eyed vision. The faults and weaknesses of the other are very much part of their love. The challenge of this reality calls forth a deeper, richer quality in their love.

It is one of the strongest elements of the Father's message to us in the Scriptures, and in the person of Jesus, that he is the supreme realist, that he is ready to accept in return the slightest movement of love from the worst of human beings. The criminal dying on the cross beside Jesus seemed to be offering little enough, as did the woman caught in the act of adultery; perhaps they were stunted people who, like the widow offering her little coin in the temple, were giving all that they had of love at the moment. The important thing is that they, the apostles with all their immaturity, and so many others who met Jesus, were accepted into the divine kingdom of love all the same.

Even more striking is the whole story of the Old Testament. Most Christians think of the early part of the Bible as past history, no longer really relevant for those who have heard the Gospel. Or they think of it as the story of man's long waiting for the Messiah, and God's patient tutoring of his people through the schoolroom days of the law; it is all this, but very much more. It is a real and present dialogue of love: right in the beginning it is a story of God forming the whole world of reality, and finding that it is all good, something to love; then the vivid picture of the uniting love of the man and the woman, of their discovery of evil, of their fear and flight, of how they hid themselves from love.

The whole long story of the Old Testament is not so much that of man's waiting for the Messiah, like a child waiting for his father, as that of a father waiting for his child, as that of God waiting for man; waiting for him to grow up in love. This is why the Old Testament is not outdated but is still part of God's message to man in the twentieth century. If we are sometimes shocked at the evil in the lives of its human characters, at their general immaturity, their petty duplicity, their revenges, their bloodthirstiness, their fear of God, their fickleness in loving, can we say that the contrasting picture of God's patient waiting, which is the other side of the Old Testament message, has no meaning for modern man? Can we, indeed, look inside ourselves and say that we do not need this part of the message any more? That we have matured in love to the point where this has no meaning for us?

If we are distressed at the Old Testament's picture of God as sometimes jealous, strict and vengeful, we might remember that not only was this the one way many of the human authors, however inspired, were able to think of God, but that, as we saw at the beginning of this article a great many modern Christians are no further in their growing up than these Jews of an older time. Perhaps all of us need to listen to the sometimes stern message of the Old Law—since the most loving fathers often seem stern until we see that they are loving—before we can understand to the full the new message of Jesus in the Gospels, and of the Spirit of Love in Pentecost and in our hearts.

So the final answer to both of our difficulties about human maturity comes clear. The message of God's love is for all men, the mature ones, and the immature. It is for the saints and for the unholy, for the sane and for the insane, for the well-balanced and for the neurotics, for all men because they are sinners, because all have a deep need for love's liberation from all that is evil and petty and infantile.

The love of the three Persons is there, waiting, for those people who are so stunted in their emotional growth that they have nothing of love to give at present; it is there in abundance for those who are growing into well-integrated maturity and are capable of warmhearted inter-personal response. For these it is a constant challenge to further growth in love—not only in the love of the Spirit, but in the love of themselves and of their brother men. For there is no limit to love; it is never possible to say that we have loved enough. We can go on and on into love, for we are then going into the deep center of reality.

Practical?

There are some who think that this is all very beautiful, but no very practical in the twentieth century. Yet love is the only practical thing in the twentieth century, or any other. Think of a boy and a girl who have fallen in love; there is a tendency for older and less mature people to laugh at them for living in an unreal world of their own. It is the laughing ones who are impractical, unreal, walking on air, for imagining that love, any love, is not important, that any human being can really live without being in love.

If we must be practical, listen to a working child psychologist lecturing to parents—he will be telling them that their children can grow only in an atmosphere of warmth, security and constant loving. Listen even to an intelligent and practical statesman talking about the bomb—he will be saying that the two sides must learn to understand and trust one another. Listen to a practical expert in the field of race relations—he will be saying that the deep root of every solution is that we must learn to love our brother man. Listen to a prison psychologist—he will be talking about men and women who are emotionally deprived, insecure, lonely, starved of love. Listen to a marriage counselor talking about broken marriages—he will be talking about men and women who lack maturity, lack the capacity to make meaningful and secure relationships, lack the ability to love. Indeed love is so practical, its need so urgent, that we might even listen to the center of all love, of all reality, telling us, "Live on in my love . . . this is my commandment that you should love one another as I have loved you."

The implications of all this for parents, for schoolteachers, for all educators, are of tremendous importance. Growth in the capacity of loving must be the central aim of all education. True education, if it is to be something more than the absorbing of useful information, learning of common skills, gaining the ability and qualifications for earning money, must be centered around the whole growth of the human person leading to the full capacity for mature adult love.

Catholic educators, in home, school and parish, must pass on to children the full Christian revelation of love contained in the whole of the Scriptures. We have seen that our view of religion, and of the whole of reality, can be stunted and dwarfed by our own emotional immaturity. It is distressing to find, again and again, graduates of Catholic schools basically ignorant of the simple, central truths of the New Testament message discussed in this article. And any teacher who has found anything new and unusual in this article would do well to set aside a few hours for the thoughtful re-reading of the whole of the New Testament. It is very easy, without periodic self-examination, to be giving to pupils a view of Christianity very similar to that outlined at the beginning of this article; a view of a strict, legalistic deity whom we serve by careful obedience in order to gain the reward of heaven, and to avoid hell. Our growth into the image of Christ by the lovepower of the Spirit seems to be overlooked, and, with it, all the challenges of responsible decision and action that are involved in our commitment of love with all three Persons.

The religious practices of school, home and parish should be arranged so that, as the child grows, there is a steady lessening of leading him by the hand to God, and a growing responsibility of personal decision. Without responsibility, there can be no growth in love. The child should be gradually allowed, even at the risks of making mistakes and wrong decisions, to think for himself and make his own decisions about daily prayers, about going to confession and communion, even about going to Mass. If he should make wrong decisions, these give the opportunity for the kind of personal religious counseling so much neglected in Christian education. The challenge of the love of the Trinity must become for the child something deeply personal involving him in love, and in the decisions and actions flowing from love. For this growth it is not sufficient for forty children to be saying together each morning, "O my God, I love you above all things."

For the same reason, the practical arrangements of discipline and authority in the Catholic school and home should be made so as to allow the child room to grow, so that there is possible for the child a steady growth in responsible action, a growth in the freedom proper to a child of our Father in heaven. Psychologists tell us that children gain their first natural knowledge of God by a reflection of the authority attitudes of their parents; it may well be that the fearful vision of a strict legalistic God, common to many Catholics, may also be a reflected image of authoritarian discipline and a passion for order and tidiness, not unknown in Catholic schools.

Finally, Catholic school teachers and priests should realize that mature parents form mature children. Parents should be treated as mature Catholics who have a clear role and responsibility not only in the everyday arranging of their home, but above all in the whole maturing and religious development of their children. If parents are treated as children, doing just what Sister, Father, and Brother tell them, responsible only for petty details, in such matters as preparation for first confession, first communion, and confirmation, they can hardly be expected to be passing on to their children mature attitudes of responsibility and decision in response to the Spirit of love.

These are only a few examples. All the factors and attitudes that go to the growth of human maturity, well outlined for us in the works of the modern psychologists, form the important and indispensable basis of Christian education. For it is within this natural growth that the Father's message to the child is heard; it is within the scope of this growth that the answering love of the child, and, eventually, of the adult Christian, can find expression.

BIOGRAPHICAL NOTES

REV. DANIEL C. MAGUIRE teaches moral theology in the Department of Religious Education of the Catholic University of America.

REV. DAVID P. O'NEILL, a pastor in New Zealand, is the author of *Priestly Celibacy and Maturity* and *Priests in Crisis, A Study in Role-Change*. The final article in this book is included in the former book in an adapted form.

PAULETTE MARTIN, who has done graduate studies at Harvard and the Sorbonne, has written articles on catechetical problems for several publications, drawn from her experience with her own children and in CCD work.

SISTER FRANCES MARY, S.L. is Religion Coordinator at St. Ferdinand's School in Florissant, Mo.

BROTHER ANDREW PANZARELLA, F.S.C. is head of the Religion Department at St. Augustine High School in Brooklyn.

REV. GERARD SLOYAN, formerly Chairman of the Department of Religious Education at The Catholic University of America, is now teaching in the Theology Department at Temple University.

CATHERINE B. KENNEDY, after several years of high school teaching experience and work with the Religion

Teachers Association in Chicago, is completing her work for an M.A. degree in Religious Education at Fordham University.

SISTER M. LORETTA KOLEY and her associates worked out the program here described in the Religion Department at Mercy High School, Omaha.

Bibliography

Ahern, Barnabas Mary. *Life in Christ.* Pamphlet. Glen Rock, N.J.: Paulist Press. An excellent summary, in scriptural terms, of the Christian life as a call to love.

Allport, Gordon W. *The Nature of Prejudice.* Abridged ed. Garden City, N.Y.: Doubleday-Anchor, 1958. A valuable aid to grow beyond prejudices.

Berne, Eric. *Games People Play.* New York: Grove Press, 1964. How we try to manipulate one another.

Cox, Harvey, ed. *The Situation Ethics Debate.* Philadelphia: The Westminster Press, 1968. Critical discussion of Joseph Fletcher's *Situation Ethics,* with a rebuttal.

Curran, Charles E. *Christian Morality Today: The Renewal of Moral Theology.* Notre Dame, Ind.: Fides Publishers, 1966. A readable presentation of the shift in present thinking.

Dubarle, Andre-Marie, O.P. *The Biblical Doctrine of Original Sin.* New York: Herder and Herder, 1964. What Scripture really teaches, and the development of this teaching in the Church.

Fromm, Erich. *The Art of Loving.* New York: Harper & Row, 1956. Brings out the essential unity of love in human beings.

———. *Man for Himself.* New York: Holt, Rinehart & Winston, 1947. The necessity of a real love of self in order to love others.

Häring, Bernard. *Toward a Christian Moral Theology.* Notre Dame, Ind.: University of Notre Dame Press, 1966.

Heschel, Abraham, J. *The Insecurity of Freedom.* New York: Farrar, Straus & Giroux, 1966. Essays on the connection between love and freedom, and belief in God.

Lepp, Ignace. *The Authentic Morality.* New York: The Macmillan Co., 1965. A very readable presentation of a personalist and Christian view of morality.

———. *The Psychology of Loving.* Baltimore: Helicon, 1963.

Monden, Louis. *Sin, Liberty and Law.* New York: Sheed & Ward, 1965. A positive explanation of the essence of morality and the development of the Christian conscience.

O'Neill, David. *About Loving.* Pamphlet, Christian Experience Series. Dayton, Ohio: Geo. A. Pflaum, 1965. A popular synthesis of psychological insights and Christian teaching on growth toward maturity in loving.

Oraison, Mark. *Love or Constraint?* Glen Rock, N.J.: Paulist Press. An aid to parents in guiding the emotional development of their children.

Paiget, Jean. *The Moral Judgment of the Child.* New York: The Free Press. A theory worked out through actual observation of children.

Rogers, Carl. *On Becoming a Person.* Boston: Houghton Mifflin, 1961. How we help one another become more fully persons.

Ryan, John Julian and Mary Perkins. *Love and Sexuality: A Christian Approach.* An attempt to bring together present thinking on love, morality, sexuality and growth in love.

Sloyan, Gerard S. *How Do I Know I'm Doing Right?* Pamphlet, Christian Experience Series. Dayton, Ohio: Geo A. Pflaum, 1967. A guide to forming a Christian conscience.